# CHILDREN'S LITERATURE IN THE K-3 MATHEMATICS CLASSROOM

## 50 ACTIVITIES BASED ON THE **COMMON CORE STATE STANDARDS** FOR MATHEMATICS

Adam Goldberg
Maria Diamantis
M.W. Penn

CHILDREN'S LITERATURE
IN THE K-3 MATHEMATICS CLASSROOM

50 ACTIVITIES BASED ON THE
**COMMON CORE STATE STANDARDS**
FOR MATHEMATICS

Written by Adam Goldberg, Ed.D., Maria Diamantis, Ed.D. and M. W. Penn

Design by Daphne Firos

———————————

Content © 2012 MathWord Press
Cover design © 2012 Daphne Firos

ISBN  978-0-9840425-2-4
Library of Congress Control Number: 2012947195

*Children's Literature in the K-3 Mathematics Classroom* is published by MathWord Press.

———————————

# TABLE OF CONTENTS

# INTRODUCTION

This is an exciting era for mathematics educators. For the first time in the history of education in our country we are approaching a national curriculum to guide us in our work and gauge students' progress: in 2010, the Common Core State Standards (CCSS) for Mathematics were released and they already have been adopted by 45 states.

The Standards represent a change in both the **content** that we will present in mathematics class and the **methods** we employ to present these topics. All Standards are explained and listed on the CCSS website: **www.corestandards.org**

In addition to **content standards** for each grade level, there are eight **practice standards** that should be interwoven throughout the curriculum to help facilitate conceptual understanding. The complete list of practice standards is also available on the website at: **www.corestandards.org/thestandards/mathematics/introduction/standards-for-mathematical-practice**

Our resource book has been created with activities that address every mathematics standard from Kindergarten through grade three. In addition, the authors have based the activities on stories from well known children's books. The integration of good children's literature into mathematics lessons is an enjoyable way to engage students and motivate them to learn. Literature-based activities also connect mathematics to the real and imaginary lives of children and strengthen their conceptual understanding.

Though other classroom tools are sometimes suggested, if you have pencil and paper, a ruler and a pair of scissors, some string and some glue, this book is all you need. The simple explanations, easy to follow directions, complete worksheets and templates in this guide will minimize preparation time, allowing you more time with students.

As you work with these activities please share your insights with us. We would appreciate your thoughts and experiences. Send all correspondence to: **handbook@mathwordpress.com**

CHAPTER 1: Activities based on

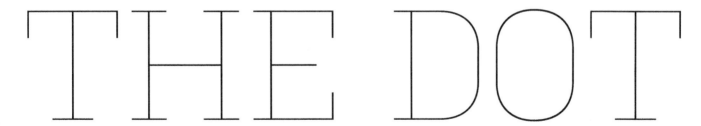

THE DOT

by Peter H. Reynolds

**3.G.1**
Understand that shapes in different categories (e.g., rhombuses, rectangles, and others) may share attributes (e.g., having four sides), and that the shared attributes can define a larger category (e.g., quadrilaterals). Recognize rhombuses, rectangles, and squares as examples of quadrilaterals, and draw examples of quadrilaterals that do not belong to any of these subcategories.

# Activity 1: 4 Dots

Read the story to the class. Give students the following grid and ask them to place four dots on the grid. You can either instruct them to place the dots at places where the lines intersect on the grid or let them draw the dots anywhere on the grid, but no more than two dots can be on any one line.

Now have them use a ruler to connect their four dots. They should use a marker so the shapes can be seen easily when displayed on a board.

Explain that the places where two lines meet at the dots they've made are called vertices of the shape they've drawn. Each dot is a vertex.

Have everyone affix the grids with their drawings to the board using either tape or magnetic tape or magnets.

Ask the class what every shape has in common. They should recognize that because they each have four vertices, each figure has four sides. Ask if they know what any shape with four sides is called. If no one offers "quadrilateral", tell them the name and write it on board.

Now ask students for a way to arrange the different shapes into a few groups. This will depend on what types of quadrilaterals students drew, but expect answers such as squares, rectangles, rhombuses, trapezoids, and/or parallelograms.

Write the classifications across a board and have students move their shape to the appropriate spot.

You will probably need a category for shapes that do not fall under typical categories listed.

Lead students into discussions such as, "Are all squares rectangles?", and "Are all rectangles squares?"

# Dot Activity Grid

## Activity 2: Big Dots and Rectangles

This activity would work best in cooperative groups of 2-4.

Give each group a "toolbox" consisting of a ruler, a piece of string and 3 copies each of the following circle and rectangle templates.

Explain to groups that their task is to begin with the first circle and rectangle and partition each into 2 equal parts. Each group should write down the unit fraction (i.e. $\frac{1}{2}$) represented by their partitions. They must be able to explain how they know that the two parts are equal.

They are then to complete the same task for 3 equal parts ($\frac{1}{3}$), and 4 equal parts ($\frac{1}{4}$).

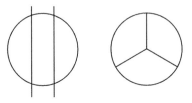

**Note that most groups will not be able to solve the 3 equal parts with the circle. This is a very difficult task. Most groups will simply use horizontal or vertical lines to split the circle, but this will not result in equal parts.

One solution involves tracing the outline of the circle with a piece of string, then using that piece of string to measure three equal segments of the circumference. Trace the entire circle with the string, divide the string into 3 equal parts and cut off one of the parts. This is $\frac{1}{3}$ of the circumference. Make a point anywhere on the circle and use the cut piece of string to measure along the circumference to the second point. Repeat the measurement from the second point to find the third point. Now use a ruler to draw line segments from those three points to the center of the circle. It should look similar to a pie chart.

When groups have completed as many tasks as they were able to accomplish, discuss whether it was easier to work with the circle or the rectangle. Have them shade in one piece of each of the 6 shapes and discuss how that represents the unit fraction they wrote.

# Circle Worksheet

We divided this circle into _____ equal parts.

Each part represents _____ of the entire circle.

We know each part is equal because _____

_____

_____

_____

_____

# Rectangle Worksheet

We divided this rectangle into _____ equal parts.

Each part represents _____ of the entire rectangle.

We know each part is equal because _____

_____

_____

_____

_____

# Activity 3: Dot Paintings

**PART 1**

After reading the book, show students a large circle. Large fraction circle manipulatives would work well here. Additionally, you can add magnetic tape to stick the circle to the board. You can even purchase large magnetic fraction circles. These are excellent for display purposes. Circles cut from construction paper also could be used.

Tell students that when Vashti became famous, she went back and found her first dot drawing. To show her gratitude to her parents and her teacher, she decided to divide that dot painting into four equal pieces. She wrote a little thank-you note on three of the four pieces for her mother, her father, and her teacher. The fourth piece she would save in her scrapbook.

Show students the circle and ask how they could divide it into 4 equal pieces. This should not be difficult for them as they should have seen this done in earlier grades.

You can either use the $\frac{1}{4}$ fraction circles or a drawing to show the circle divided into 4 equal pieces. Point to one of the pieces and ask students what fraction of the whole circle this represents. When a student offers the answer $\frac{1}{4}$, write it on the board. Be sure to write it as 1 over 4. It is much easier for students to think of the fraction as numerator over denominator when it is written vertically. Additionally, this will make it much easier to perform operations on fractions in later grades.

Point to the denominator 4 and ask students what that number represents. You are looking for the answer that it represents the number of equal pieces of the dot after Vashti divided the dot into four pieces. Now point to the 1 and again ask what it represents. This numerator represents the 1 piece out of the four that was selected.

Draw the following circle on the board and point to any of the four "pieces". Ask if that piece represents one fourth of the circle. You want students to recognize that in order to discuss fractions, we must be dealing with equal-size pieces.

Now, explain that we are going to go back to our first example and look at the pieces Vashti gave to her parents. Because she has two parents, they received a total of two pieces. Ask students what fraction they can write to show the portion her parents received. They should find the fraction $\frac{2}{4}$. For reinforcement, ask students what the 2 and then the 4 represent.

Now, group together the two pieces that represent her mother's and father's gifts and compare those with the two pieces that are left. Ask students for another fraction that can represent the two pieces that are together. It should be easy for students to see that we can also use $\frac{1}{2}$ to represent the situation. (At this point, you may want to use $\frac{1}{2}$ sized fraction circles.)

Say that Vashti would like to divide the circle into 6 equal pieces. Explain that we can also use a number line to represent these fractional pieces. In this case we would want to break the space between 0 and 1 on a number line into 6 equal segments.

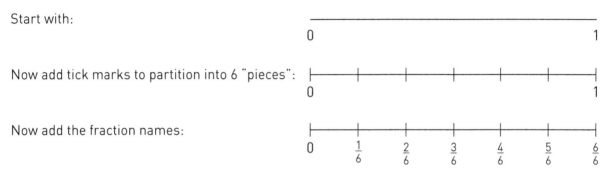

Start with:

0                                                                1

Now add tick marks to partition into 6 "pieces":

0                                                                1

Now add the fraction names:

0    $\frac{1}{6}$    $\frac{2}{6}$    $\frac{3}{6}$    $\frac{4}{6}$    $\frac{5}{6}$    $\frac{6}{6}$

Ask students questions such as "What is another name for $\frac{3}{6}$?" You may want to ask if anyone knows another name for $\frac{2}{6}$. Some students may see that this can also be thought of as $\frac{1}{3}$. You should also point out that another name for 1 is $\frac{6}{6}$. Explain that if you had a pizza that was cut into 6 pieces and you ate all 6 pieces, you would have eaten the whole pizza.

Once you feel students are comfortable with the circle model, explain to them that a famous artist named Mondrian has painted a series of paintings using rectangles. You can find more on Mondrian and his work at: **www.artcyclopedia.com/artists/mondrian_piet.html**

Ask students to represent the fraction $\frac{1}{8}$ both on a rectangle and on a number line.

## PART 2
Once students are comfortable with the number line, the standard circle and rectangle as models for fractions, you can move to pattern blocks. Give students some of the yellow hexagons, blue rhombuses, red trapezoids, and green triangles. (Cut pattern blocks from colored paper if you have none available.)

Explain to them that the yellow hexagon is going to represent 1. Ask them to find fractional names for each of the other three pieces. They should see that the green triangle would be $\frac{1}{6}$, the blue rhombus would be $\frac{1}{3}$, and the red trapezoid would be $\frac{1}{2}$.

If students are able to see this conceptually, you might want to try a more difficult example. In this case, let 2 hexagons represent 1 whole. Now the red trapezoid is only $\frac{1}{4}$ and the blue rhombus is only $\frac{1}{6}$ of the total area. You can also ask about the green triangle which would be $\frac{1}{12}$.

## PART 3
The Tangram Extension Worksheet (pages 13-14) can be used as an extension or as differentiation of this activity.

# Dot and Rectangle Paintings Worksheet

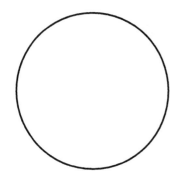

1. For this circle, show how you would represent $\frac{1}{4}$.

2a. For this rectangle, show how you would represent $\frac{2}{6}$.

2b. On this rectangle, show how you would represent $\frac{1}{3}$.

2c. What do you notice about the pieces in 2a and 2b?

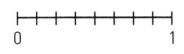

3a. Mark $\frac{6}{8}$ on the number line.

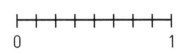

3b. Now show $\frac{3}{4}$ on the number line.

# Tangram Extension Worksheet

Use all seven pieces of your tangram set to cover the square below:

Answer the following questions based on the tangrams:

1. If the square was equal to one whole, what fraction of it would the large triangle cover? Explain how you found your answer.

What fraction of the square would the medium triangle cover?

2. Now assume that the large triangle represents 1 whole. What fraction would each of the other pieces cover?

Small Triangle _____   Medium Triangle _____

Square _____   Parallelogram _____

# Tangram Template

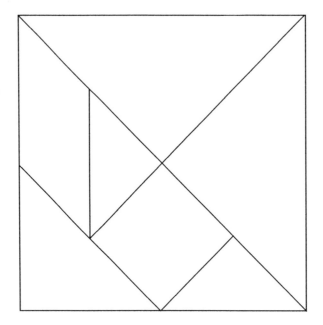

**3.MD.5**
Recognize area as an attribute of plane figures and understand concepts of area measurement.
- A square with side length 1 unit, called "a unit square," is said to have "one square unit" of area, and can be used to measure area.
- A plane figure which can be covered without gaps or overlaps by n unit squares is said to have an area of n square units.

**3.MD.6**
Measure areas by counting unit squares (square cm, square m, square in, square ft, and improvised units).

**3.MD.7**
Relate area to the operations of multiplication and addition.
- Find the area of a rectangle with whole-number side lengths by tiling it, and show that the area is the same as would be found by multiplying the side lengths.

# Activity 4: Dots on the Geoboard
## Measuring Area with Unit Squares

After reading the book, ask students to imagine a painting with rows and columns of dots. Now show them a geoboard and explain how this is similar to the rows and columns of dots.

Give each student a geoboard and some elastic bands. If you do not have access to actual geoboards, this activity can be done as a demonstration using virtual geoboards. Geoboards may be found on the web at the National Library of Virtual Manipulatives:

**http://nlvm.usu.edu/en/nav/topic_t_3.html**

or on NCTM's web site:

**www.nctm.org/standards/content.aspx?id=25007)**

Or use the **Geoboard Template** on page 21.

First, construct a 1x1 square as a demonstration to the students. Tell students that each side of this square is 1 unit and the area of the square is 1 square unit. Explain to students that we call this a unit square. Remind students that area represents the amount of space enclosed by the shape; also remind them that area is expressed in square units.

Now construct a 2x2 square. Ask students how long each side is now. Their answer should be 2 units. Ask them what the area is; they can count the unit squares. Students should understand that the square is comprised of 4 unit squares so the area is 4 square units.

Now have students construct a 3x3 square. Ask them both the length of each side and the area. Ask if they see a relationship between the length of the side and the area. If they do not see the relationship, do not immediately offer it.

Now, ask the students to construct a 2x4 rectangle on their geoboards. Ask them to count the length of each side and determine the total area of the rectangle. Again, ask if they see any relationship between the lengths of the sides and the area.

Have students work on the following worksheet. By the end of the lesson, students should understand that they have two ways to find the area of squares and rectangles. One way is to simply count the number of unit squares (1x1) the shape encompasses; the other way is to multiply the lengths of the sides.

# Geoboard Worksheet

1. Construct a 4 x 4 square on your geoboard.
    a) Count the number of unit squares to determine the area.
    b) What is the length of one side?
    c) Multiply the answer in (b) by itself. Is this the same answer as (a)?


2. Construct a 3 x 2 rectangle on your geoboard.
    a) Count the number of unit squares to determine the area.
    b) What is the length of the longer side of the rectangle?
    c) What is the length of the shorter side of the rectangle?
    d) Multiply the answer in (b) by the answer in (c). Is this the same
       answer as (a)?


3. Construct a 1 x 5 rectangle on your geoboard.
    a) Count the number of unit squares to determine the area.
    b) What is the length of the longer side of the rectangle?
    c) What is the length of the shorter side of the rectangle?
    d) Multiply the answer in (b) by the answer (c). Is this the same answer as (a)?


4. Based on these results, develop a formula or a rule to find the area of squares
and rectangles.

## 3.MD.5

Recognize area as an attribute of plane figures and understand concepts of area measurement.
- A square with side length 1 unit, called "a unit square," is said to have "one square unit" of area, and can be used to measure area.
- A plane figure which can be covered without gaps or overlaps by n unit squares is said to have an area of n square units.

## 3.MD.6

Measure areas by counting unit squares (square cm, square m, square in, square ft, and improvised units).

## 3.MD.7

Relate area to the operations of multiplication and addition.
- Find the area of a rectangle with whole-number side lengths by tiling it, and show that the area is the same as would be found by multiplying the side lengths.
- Multiply side lengths to find areas of rectangles with whole-number side lengths in the context of solving real world and mathematical problems, and represent whole-number products as rectangular areas in mathematical reasoning.
- Recognize area as additive. Find areas of rectilinear figures by decomposing them into non-overlapping rectangles and adding the areas of the non-overlapping parts, applying this technique to solve real world problems.

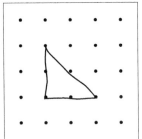

Figure A          Figure B

# Activity 5: More Dots on the Geoboard

### PART 1

This activity builds on the previous geoboard activity. In this activity, we go beyond areas of rectangles and squares and examine the areas of triangles and shapes that are composed of rectangles and triangles.

Ask students to create a 2x4 rectangle on their geoboards.

Remember that if you do not have access to actual geoboards, this activity can be done as a demonstration using virtual geoboards. Geoboards may be found on the web at the National Library of Virtual Manipulatives:

http://nlvm.usu.edu/en/nav/topic_t_3.html

or on NCTM's web site:

www.nctm.org/standards/content.aspx?id=25007)

Or use the **Geoboard Template** on page 21.

Now ask students to create a triangle that is exactly half of the rectangle they have on their boards. Ask them to estimate the area of this triangle. Have students explain why they feel their answer is correct. Students should determine that the triangle will be exactly half of the area of the rectangle. Since the rectangle has an area of 8 square units, the triangle has an area of 4 square units. Explain that this is exactly how we are going to find the area of triangles—by finding the rectangle that is twice its size.

It is helpful to remind students that some of these rectangles may be squares and that squares are rectangles with 4 equal sides.

Also, in this lesson we are only looking at right triangles. They are triangles that can easily be seen as half of a rectangle. In later grades, students will examine the relationship of other types of triangles.

Now, construct a right triangle in which each leg is 2 units long. It should resemble **Figure A**.

Ask students to recreate it either on geoboards or graph paper and, once they have constructed it, try to determine its area. If they do not construct the square on their own, lead them to complete the larger square and see that because this square is 2 units by 2 units it has an area of 4 square units. Because the triangle is $\frac{1}{2}$ the area of the square, it would have an area of 2 square units (**Figure B**).

As a final practice, ask students to find the area of a right triangle that has legs of 3 units and 4 units by first constructing the triangle and then constructing a rectangle by adding a second triangle. The answer they should find for the area of the triangle is 6 square units.

At this point some students should notice it is easier to multiply the lengths of the sides of the rectangles to determine the area. In the case of the triangle, though, you must also divide by two, or cut the area in half. This division leads to the area formula for triangles:

$A = \frac{1}{2} b \times h$, where b is the length of the base and h is the length of the height.

Remember that at this grade level, it is not necessary for students to be exposed to this formula. If some students reach this conclusion organically through the lesson that's great, but you do not need to give them the formula.


## PART 2

Explain to students that they have been selected to oversee the school's new garden. However, first they must determine how much land they have to work with.

Show students the following arrangement on the geoboard and explain that, instead of each length being 1 unit, it is now 1 meter.

Remember that if you do not have access to actual geoboards, this activity can be done as a demonstration using virtual geoboards.
Geoboards may be found on the web at the National Library of Virtual Manipulatives:

http://nlvm.usu.edu/en/nav/topic_t_3.html

or on NCTM's web site:

www.nctm.org/standards/content.aspx?id=25007)

Or use the **Geoboard Template** on page 21.

Ask students to find the area of the garden. On the following worksheet, they are asked to explain how they found their answer.

You should expect a variety of answers. Some students may break the shape into different rectangles and find the areas of each rectangle and then add the areas together; some will just count the number of unit squares in the irregular shape; some students might even realize that the shape comprises all but 3 squares on a geoboard and so subtract 16 – 3 to get the answer of 13 square meters.

# School Garden Worksheet

Congratulations! You have been chosen to oversee the new school garden.

Your first task is to determine how much land you have available to use. The geoboard below shows the shape of the garden. The length between each dot is 1 meter.

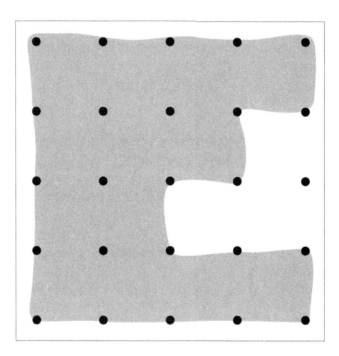

## What is the area of the garden?

Carefully explain your answer including any addition, multiplication or subtraction that you did.

# Geoboard Template

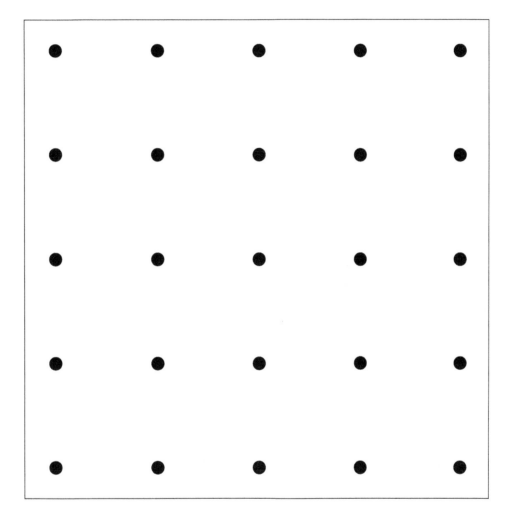

CHAPTER 2: Activities based on

# THE GIVING TREE

by Shel Silverstein

**K.G.1**
Describe objects in the environment using names of shapes, and describe the relative positions of these objects using terms such as *above, below, beside, in front of, behind, and next to.*

**K.G.3**
Identify shapes as two-dimensional (lying in a plane, "flat") or three-dimensional ("solid").

**K.G.5**
Model shapes in the world by building shapes from components (e.g., sticks and clay balls) and drawing shapes.

**K.G.6**
Compose simple shapes to form larger shapes. *For example, "Can you join these two triangles with full sides touching to make a rectangle?"*

# Activity 1: The Shape of Trees

You will need one copy of the book to read to the class and construction paper, scissors and glue, and copies of the following shape template for each student or group of students.

After you read the story, give children a shape template and have them create 'trees' by cutting out and gluing various shapes onto the construction paper. They can use each shape many times.

Ask each child to name the shapes they used in their tree.

Now discuss differences between the 2-dimensional shapes they used to make the trees and the 3-dimensional shapes of real trees. Walk outside and write down qualities/characteristics of real, three dimensional trees. Discuss the names of some of the parts of real trees: the trunks are round and high like huge pencils or "cylinders"; some trees look like triangles from a distance, or upside-down ice-cream "cones"; the tops of some trees are round, like balls or "spheres". Ask about placement of trunk, leaves and branches: leaves above the trunk; trunk below the leaves; etc.

As an extension, you might have children create trees using modeling clay, play-dough or things like straws and cotton balls.

# The Shape of Trees Templates

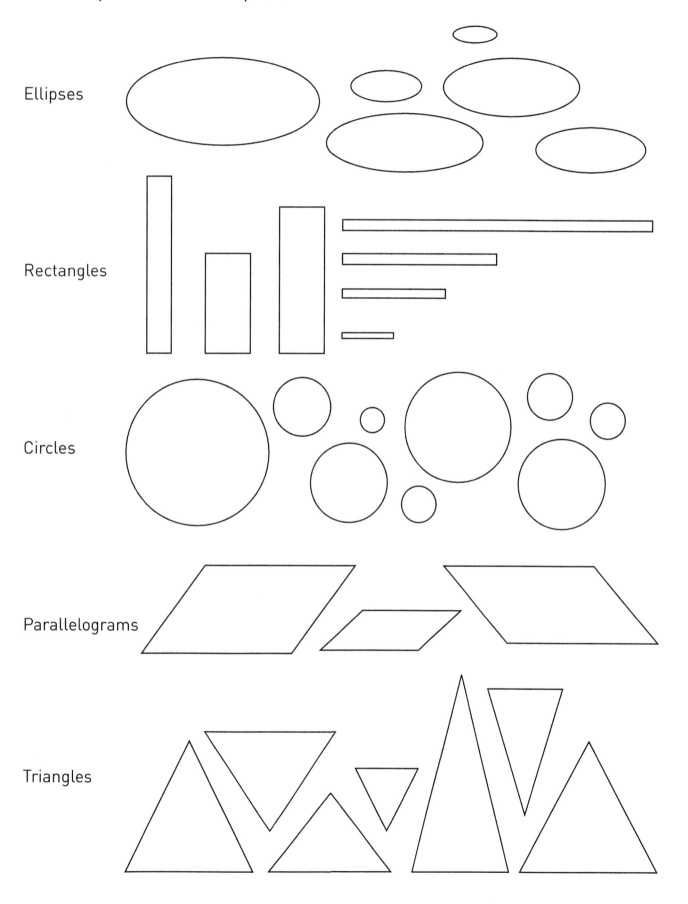

Ellipses

Rectangles

Circles

Parallelograms

Triangles

**1.MD.1**
Order three objects by length; compare the lengths of two objects indirectly by using a third object.

**1.MD.2**
Express the length of an object as a whole number of length units, by laying multiple copies of a shorter object (the length unit) end to end; understand that the length measurement of an object is the number of same-size length units that span it with no gaps or overlaps. *Limit to contexts where the object being measured is spanned by a whole number of length units with no gaps or overlaps..*

**1.OA.6**
Add and subtract within 20, demonstrating fluency for addition and subtraction within 10.

# Activity 2: Tree Lengths

You will need a copy of the book to read to the class and a copy of the worksheets for each student.

In this activity children use the length of one object to approximate the length of another.

Read the book. After discussing the story, compare the height of the tree to the height of the boy. Ask students which is taller. Give students the worksheets. Students should cut out the boy, tree, branch, and apple on the first page. They will answer the questions on the second sheet based on measurements made using the lengths of the cutouts.

# Tree Lengths Worksheet Page 2

1. Which is taller, the boy or the branch? Explain why you think so. Measure to see if your estimate is correct.

2. How many branches tall is the tree? If the height of the branch is actually 3 feet, how tall is the tree?

3. How many apples tall is the branch? Show a picture explaining how you found your answer.

4. How many apples tall is the tree? How did you find your answer?

5. If you were to measure your desk using the tree, about how many trees wide would it be? Measure and see how close you came.

# TEACHER'S NOTES

# Activity 3: Apple Orchards

## PART 1

You will need a copy of the book to read to the class and copies of the following diagrams.

After reading the book, begin by showing students the first diagram of an apple orchard. The shaded region represents the portion of the orchard that is currently growing apples.

Ask students how many sections the orchard has been separated into. They should recognize that it has been partitioned into four sections.

Discuss the four sections using the word fourths. Ask students how many fourths there are in the entire drawing. They should answer that there are 4 fourths. Point out that 4 fourths make up one whole.

Now, ask what fraction of the orchard has been used for apples. Lead students to associate fourths with the fraction $\frac{1}{4}$. Stress that the sections are equal.

Next, show them the diagram of the second orchard and ask if the shaded section growing apples still represents $\frac{1}{4}$ of the orchard. They should decide that it does not. Discuss their answer, leading them to understand that when we talk about fractions, we must have equal-sized pieces. In order to divide anything into fourths, each of the four pieces must be the same size.

Now, have students look at the third diagram.

Ask students to complete these sentences:
This circle has _____ equal pieces.
The shaded part represents the fraction _____.

# Orchard Diagrams

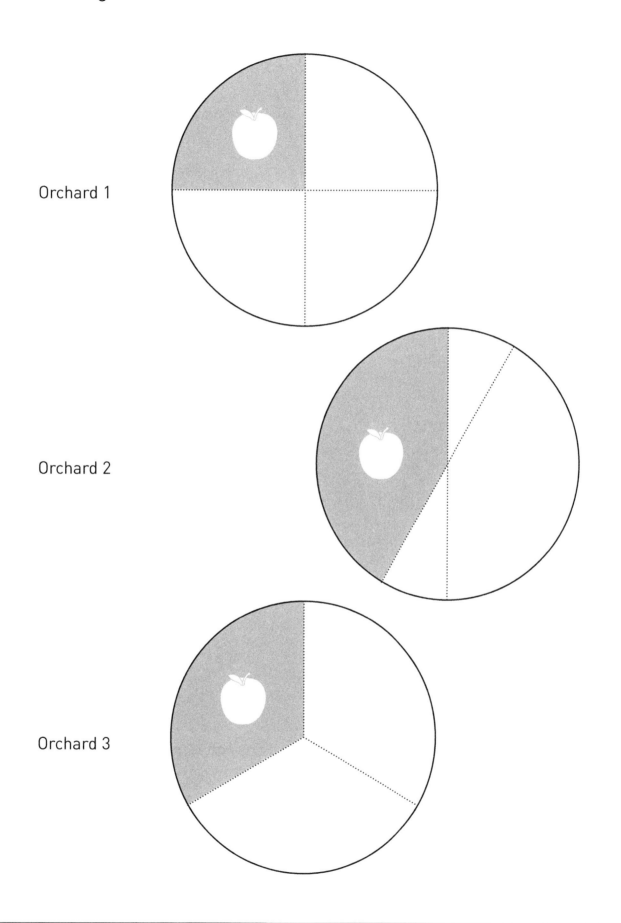

Orchard 1

Orchard 2

Orchard 3

# Apple Orchard Worksheet

On this worksheet, the area of the orchard filled with apple trees is shaded.

For each of the following orchards, explain what fraction of the orchard is filled with apple trees.

1. The area planted with apples:

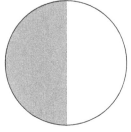

2. The area planted with apples:

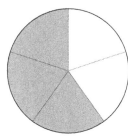

3. The area planted with apples:

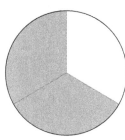

4. The area planted with apples:

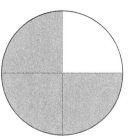

5. Compare the shaded parts of the orchard diagrams in questions 2 and 4. Which orchard has more of its area growing apples?

How would you write an inequality to show this?

# TEACHER'S NOTES

## Activity 4: Apple Orchards continued

**PART 2**

In this activity students will create orchards and plant anything they choose. Let them be creative. For example, if they want to plant bicycles, that's great.

Make a copy of the following Orchard Template Page for each student or group of students. Each orchard template is divided into halves, thirds or fourths. To create their orchards, students will choose three different 'orchards' from the circle and rectangle templates, one of either a rectangle or a circle template for each of the three fractional representations. For each orchard shape they chose, they should cut out the template and color in either $\frac{1}{2}$, $\frac{1}{3}$, or $\frac{1}{4}$.

On the My Orchard Worksheet, they are to glue their colored 'orchard' section onto the sheet. They should write the fractional name for the colored the portion that they will plant. Then they can write a few sentences explaining what it is they are planting.

When they complete their orchards, they can share them with other students.

# Orchard Template Page

### Orchard 1

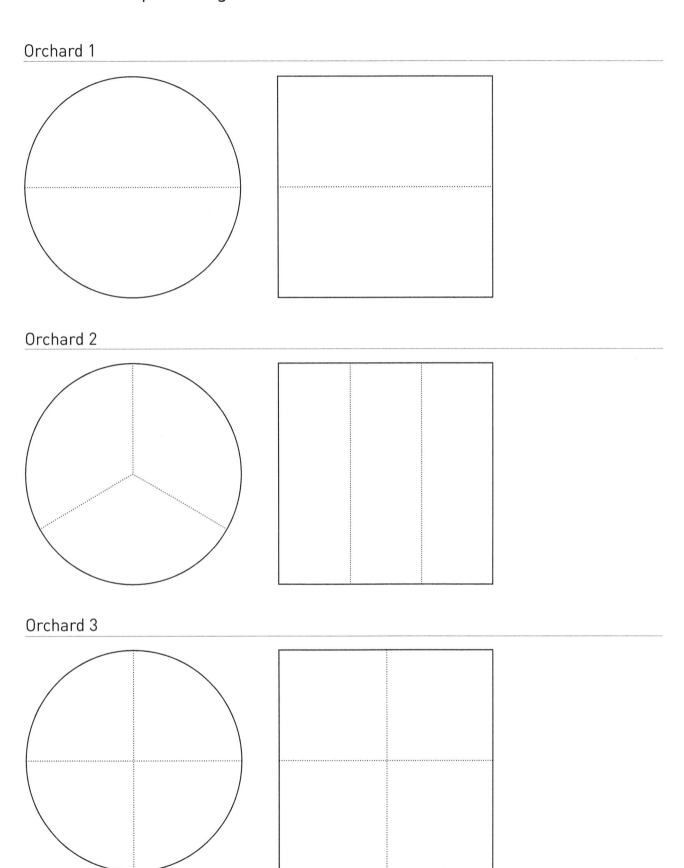

### Orchard 2

### Orchard 3

# My Orchard Worksheet

1. Glue your orchard here.

In my orchard, I planted_____.

The fraction _____ represents the part of my orchard that is planted with _____.

2. Glue your orchard here.

In my orchard, I planted_____.

The fraction _____ represents the part of my orchard that is planted with _____.

3. Glue your orchard here.

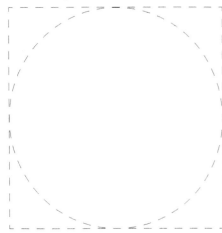

In my orchard, I planted_____.

The fraction _____ represents the part of my orchard that is planted with _____.

**2.OA.1**
Use addition and subtraction within 100 to solve one- and two-step word problems involving situations of adding to, taking from, putting together, taking apart, and comparing, with unknowns in all positions, e.g., by using drawings and equations with a symbol for the unknown number to represent the problem.

**2.MD.5**
Use addition and subtraction within 100 to solve word problems involving lengths that are given in the same units, e.g., by using drawings (such as drawings of rulers) and equations with a symbol for the unknown number to represent the problem.

## Activity 5: Tree Equations

You will need one copy of the book to read to the class and a copy of the following worksheet for each student.

After reading the story, have children solve the following problems. Ask them to show their work and explain how they found each answer.

# Tree Equations Worksheet

1. Imagine the **Giving Tree** was 34 feet tall. If the boy was only 4 feet tall, how much taller would the tree be?

2. The boy measured one of the leaves that fell from the **Giving Tree** and it was $7\frac{1}{2}$ inches long. On the ruler below, draw a line that shows exactly how long the leaf was.

3. Often it is easier to work with centimeters than it is to work with inches. $7\frac{1}{2}$ inches is about 19 centimeters. Show where that would be on the centimeter ruler below:

4. When the boy became an old man and cut down the tree to make a boat, all that was left was a stump. When he returned he wanted to know how much of the tree he had cut down. He remembered that at one time the tree was 34 feet tall and now the stump was only 2 feet tall.

He wrote the following equation: 34 - ☐ = 2.

What does the ☐ represent in this problem? What value should we put in ☐?

Could the man also have written: ☐ + 2 = 34?

What does the ☐ represent in this problem? What value should we put in ☐?

5. Measure two different objects in your class. Write an equation like one of the equations in number 4 and use it to find out how much bigger one of the objects is than the other.

CHAPTER 3: Activities based on

# GUESS HOW MUCH I LOVE YOU

by Sam McBratney

# Activity 1: Measure Up

### PART 1

After reading the story, begin by asking students to show you how much Little Nutbrown Hare loved Big Nutbrown Hare. They should all hold their arms out wide.

Now have students measure their arm-spans with a piece of string. They should work in pairs or groups to measure each other. After they have measured their arm-span with the string, they next use the string to compare the length of the span to their height by holding the string at the top of their head and letting it fall to the floor.

Ask students to make an observation. They should recognize that the length of their arm-span is almost identical to their height.

### PART 2

Now give each pair or group of students three common but different-sized objects – such as index cards, blocks, plastic spoons, Cuisenaire rods, popsicle sticks – to use as tools for measuring.

Have students work together to measure their height and fill out the following worksheet using these nonstandard measurement tools. You should tell them which tool to use for object 1, 2, and 3 so the worksheets are consistent. That is, if index cards are one of the objects, have everyone use index cards for object 1.

Have students create a graph on the grid that follows showing the three different measurements. Have them properly label the title of the graph and then label both axes and set up an appropriate scale on the vertical axis. You can have students post their graphs around the room and ask questions such as: Which measuring tool always had the largest number? Was this always true (consistent among all the groups)? Why?

# Measure Up Worksheet

Object 1: _____    Object 2: _____    Object 3: _____

I was this many _____ tall: _____
                    (object 1)

I was this many _____ tall: _____
                    (object 2)

I was this many _____ tall: _____
                    (object 3)

My Graph:

# Activity 2: Time for Bed

Have students complete the following activities.

For further exploration or as a model, visit the National Library of Virtual Manipulatives:

**http://nlvm.usu.edu/**

and click on Measurement (Grades 3-5). There are three TIME manipulatives:

Time - Analog and Digital Clocks
Time - Match Clocks
Time - What Time Will It Be?

# Time for Bed Worksheet

After hugging Big Nutbrown Hare, it was time for Little Nutbrown Hare to go to bed. His bedtime is 7:30. Can you draw arrows on the clock to show 7:30?

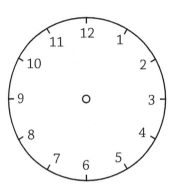

The following clock shows what time it was when Little Nutbrown Hare woke up. What time does it read?

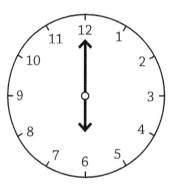

Little Nutbrown Hare always eats lunch at 11:30. Where would the arrows be at 11:30?

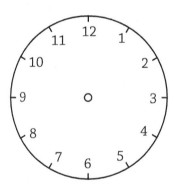

How would 11:30 look on a digital clock?

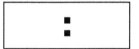

**1.OA.3**
Apply properties of operations as strategies to add and subtract.² *Examples: If 8 + 3 = 11 is known, then 3 + 8 = 11 is also known. (Commutative property of addition.) To add 2 + 6 + 4, the second two numbers can be added to make a ten, so 2 + 6 + 4 = 2 + 10 = 12. (Associative property of addition.)*

**1.OA.4**
Understand subtraction as an unknown-addend problem. *For example, subtract 10 – 8 by finding the number that makes 10 when added to 8. Add and subtract within 20.*

**1.OA.6**
Add and subtract within 20, demonstrating fluency for addition and subtraction within 10. Use strategies such as counting on; making ten (e.g., 8 + 6 = 8 + 2 + 4 = 10 + 4 = 14); decomposing a number leading to a ten (e.g., 13 – 4 = 13 – 3 – 1 = 10 – 1 = 9); using the relationship between addition and subtraction (e.g., knowing that 8 + 4 = 12, one knows 12 – 8 = 4); and creating equivalent but easier or known sums (e.g., adding 6 + 7 by creating the known equivalent 6 + 6 + 1 = 12 + 1 = 13).

# Activity 3: Adding and Subtracting Hugs

### PART 1

After reading the story, tell the students that Little Nutbrown Hare sometimes counted how many hugs he got. Tell them that one day he had gotten 6 hugs and then he got 3 more. Ask how many hugs he would have gotten altogether.

When they find the answer of 9 hugs, write the addition statement 6 + 3 = 9 on board.

Now ask how many hugs he would have gotten if he first got 3 hugs and then got 6 more. Allow students to solve the problem with any method they feel comfortable using. After someone answers 9, write 3 + 6 = 9 on board.

Ask students to examine the two number statements and discuss the answers.

Now ask if they think that adding up the same two numbers in a different order will always result in the same sum (answer). Ask how they can check. If no students suggest selecting other pairs of numbers, use 8 and 3 to show that 8 + 3 = 11 and 3 + 8 = 11. Continue until the class has selected and checked several different pairs.

Have students make posters representing the addition of two objects and write the two number sentences on the poster. You can either have them draw the objects, cut the objects out of a template, or print the objects out on a computer.

The following chart illustrates the commutative property:

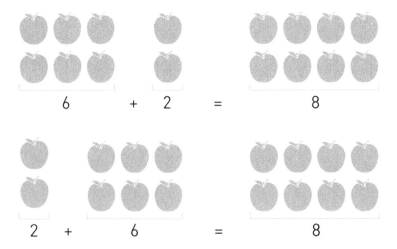

## PART 2

This is a variation of the game "I'm thinking of a number".

First, write the subtraction equation 10 - 3 = 7 either on the board, the computer (if using a projector), or an overhead projector. Cover the equation so students cannot see it. Now, tell them you are thinking of a number that when added to 7 will give the sum of 10. Let them find the answer of 3.

Show them your equation and tell them one way to solve subtraction problems is to try to find the missing number [addend]. Explain that 7 + 3 is 10, so 10 – 3 = 7.

Now, have students work with a partner. Have them take turns writing down a subtraction equation. They will tell their partner that they are thinking of a number that when added to __ the sum is ___. From this, the partner must solve the problem by finding the number that fits the equation.

**2.MD.2**
Measure the length of an object twice, using length units of different lengths for the two measurements; describe how the two measurements relate to the size of the unit chosen.

**2.MD.3**
Estimate lengths using units of inches, feet, centimeters, and meters.

**2.MD.6**
Represent whole numbers as lengths from 0 on a number line diagram with equally spaced points corresponding to the numbers 0, 1, 2, ..., and represent whole-number sums and differences within 100 on a number line diagram.

# Activity 4: Hallway Lengths

Start by showing students a yardstick and a meter stick. If you don't have either of them, you can cut a long, thin piece of paper or a piece of string or yarn to the correct lengths.

Students should stretch their arms out like Little Nut Brown Hare and measure from the finger tips of one hand to finger tips of the other using lengths of string or yarn. They should then compare their arm span to a meter stick and a yard stick. Ask which measurement yields a larger number.

Take students into the hallway or an empty gymnasium and ask them to estimate how many yards and then how many meters they think the length of the room will be.

Assign pairs or groups of students to make an exact measurement using both the yardstick and the meter stick. Each group can measure using both depending on time and resources. You also can either have them round to the nearest whole unit or nearest half-unit.

When you come back to class have students share their results. There will invariably be a small amount of difference. You can discuss human error or round-off error with them at this point.

As a final activity, have students label their results on a number line. The number line should be labeled from 0 to an appropriate number depending on what you chose to measure.

Have students make a mark at the appropriate number of meters and another at the appropriate number of yards. Have them subtract to find out how many more yards there were than meters.

Now you can discuss the reasons why when students measure the same length using both meters and yards, there are always more yards than meters. Students should recognize that there are more yards than meters because yards are smaller units and therefore there will be more yards for the same measurement.

# Activity 5: Arm Span

You will need tape measures and poster board or rolls of paper.

Have students work in groups of 3 or 4, arranging it so that there is a mixture of different heights within each group.

Ask each group to measure all of their arm spans. They are going to stretch their arms out like Little Nut Brown Hare and measure from the finger tips of one hand to finger tips of the other. For ease of measurement, have them use centimeters instead of inches.

Once they have completed the measurements, have them add all the measurements together using any method. Give each group poster board or a roll of paper to illustrate how they got their answer. Have each of the groups come up and explain their illustration.

You may also want to have manipulatives available for groups that want to use them. For example, groups could use base-10 blocks to add the lengths together. This would allow for an excellent discussion of regrouping.

After each group has presented, you can give the class a bonus question: Find the total length of the arm spans of the entire class. If they work in groups, each group would have to add all of the groups' totals together. This could provide excellent way to share and practice different strategies they have seen.

CHAPTER 4: Activities based on

# IF YOU GIVE A MOUSE A COOKIE

by Felicia Bond

**1.G.3**
Partition circles and rectangles into two and four equal shares, describe the shares using the words *halves, fourths,* and *quarters,* and use the phrases *half of, fourth of,* and *quarter of.* Describe the whole as two of, or four of the shares. Understand for these examples that decomposing into more equal shares creates smaller shares.

# Activity 1: Pieces of Cookies

After reading the book, explain to students that they are going to break a cookie equally between them and the mouse. Hand out a cookie circle cut-out to each student or group of students. Also, have available scissors, a ruler, and a pencil.

Explain to students that they should cut the circle into 2 equal pieces. On each piece they should write the word 'half'.

Walk around and check that everyone is correctly cutting the circle in half. When students have completed the task, have them go around the room and examine other students' work. Ask for an observation. They should notice that everyone's two pieces look the same. That is, no matter how you cut the circle in half, each piece should be the same size.

Now explain that instead of a circular cookie, you decided to make a rectangular brownie. Give the students the brownie rectangle and ask them to again cut in half. Have them write "half" on each piece. Unlike the circle, there will be different ways to partition a rectangle into halves. Some students may choose a vertical cut; some a horizontal cut; some a diagonal cut or something even more intricate.

Have students share their results. You may want to have them post their halves on the board grouped by the way they made the cuts. Now give students another rectangle and ask them to divide it into 4 equal pieces. Have them write the word "fourth" on each piece. Again, there may be some creative ways that students find to divide the rectangle into fourths.

Ensure that the four pieces are the same size. It is extremely important in first grade that any exposure to fractional pieces leads students to come away with the understanding that in order to discuss halves and fourths or any other fractions, we must be dealing with equal-sized pieces.

# Circle and Rectangle (cookie and brownie) templates

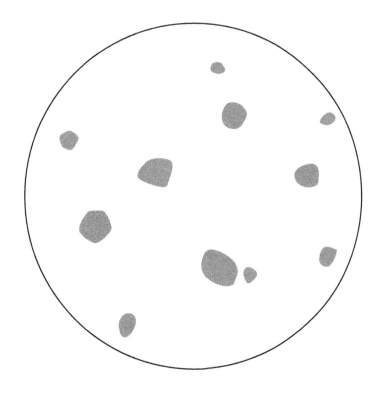

**1.OA.7**
Understand the meaning of the equal sign, and determine if equations involving addition and subtraction are true or false. For example, which of the following equations are true and which are false? $6 = 6$, $7 = 8 - 1$, $5 + 2 = 2 + 5$, $4 + 1 = 5 + 2$.

# Activity 2: The Truth About Cookies

After reading the story, draw the following two cookies on the board:

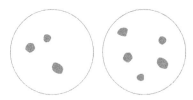

Now ask how many chocolate chips are in the first cookie and how many are in the second cookie.

After students tell you there are 3 and 5, write $3 + 5 = 9$ on the board. Ask them to study the equation. Ask them if this is correct or incorrect.

While they study the equation, ask students what the equal sign means. They should understand that the equal sign means that whatever is to the left of an equal sign has the same value as that to the right.

So, $3 + 5 = 8$ not 9. Tell students that $3 + 5 = 9$ would be false.

Now write the following three problems and ask students if they are true or false and have them explain each answer:
1) $6 + 5 = 11$    2) $9 - 7 = 1$    3) $5 + 2 = 1 + 6$

Give students this word problem and ask them to first write an equation modeling the situation and then decide if the equation is true or false: **Shannon ate 6 cookies last week and 5 cookies this week, so she has eaten 12 cookies in all.**

Students should first write the equation that is being modeled: **6 + 5 = 12**. They then must recognize that it is **FALSE**.

Now ask them to write the correct equation. Their correct equation should read: $6 + 5 = 11$

As a follow-up activity, give students four different dominoes. Have them create four true / false questions based on the dominoes. For example, if I had the domino shown to the left:

One possible true statement could be: $6 + 4 = 10$; a false statement could be $6 + 4 = 8$. Another true statement could be $10 - 4 = 6$; a false statement could be $10 + 4 = 12$.

Family Math: You may want to have students take their worksheets home and have their parents "play" a game of selecting the true statements.

# True or False Worksheet

Domino 1:

True addition statement:                    False addition statement:

_____

Domino 2:

True addition statement:                    False addition statement:

_____

Domino 3:

True subtraction statement:                  False subtraction statement:

_____

Domino 4:

True subtraction statement:                  False subtraction statement:

_____

# Activity 3: Adding Cookies

All students should have access to manipulatives for this activity. Round plastic chips or rounds cut from construction paper would be perfect representations of cookies. One possibility is to cut out circles and have students color them to replicate different kinds of cookies. You can even laminate them to make them even more durable.

Have students model the following situation:
The mouse's plate had 5 cookies on it. After putting more cookies on the plate, the mouse had 8 cookies. How many more cookies did he add?

Before trying to solve the problem, have students model the appropriate equation: $5 + ? = 8$

Stress the fact that we used the **?** to represent the part that we don't know and will solve for.

Now have them count how many more "cookies" they would need to add to get to 8 cookies.

Write the equation $12 - ? = 9$. Ask students to think of a story about cookies that would fit that equation. The important point is that students are able to come up with a situation in which they begin with 12 things, take ? away and end with 9.

Now ask students to solve for ? using their manipulatives. They should start with 12 and count the number they had to take away to get to 9.

You may have to repeat this activity with different numbers until students are comfortable with both addition and subtraction equations.

Have students complete the following worksheet.

# Worksheet for Adding Up Cookies

1. Isobel and Madelynn made cookies for their mouse friends. They made 12 chocolate chip cookies and 5 oatmeal raisin cookies. How many cookies did they make? Write an equation using **?** for the number you must solve for.

2. The next day they made 14 cookies. After they gave some cookies to Isobel's dad to take to work, they had 8 cookies left. How many cookies did they give to Isobel's dad? Write an equation using **?** for the number you must solve for.

3. The mice were so thankful for the cookies that they decided to bring pieces of fruit for the girls to eat. They brought some oranges and some apples. Altogether, they brought 13 pieces of fruit. If 4 were apples, how many were oranges? Write an equation using **?** for the number you must solve for.

4. Isobel ate one orange and Madelynn ate two apples. How many apples were left? Write an equation to solve this.

5. How many oranges were left? Write an equation to solve this.

6. How many pieces of fruit did they eat? Write an equation to solve this.

7. How many pieces of fruit were left? Write an equation to solve this.

# Activity 4: How Long Did That Take?

Have students complete the following activities.

For further exploration or as a model, visit the National Library of Virtual Manipulatives:

**nlvm.usu.edu**

and click on Measurement (Grades 3-5). There are three TIME manipulatives:

Time - Analog and Digital Clocks
Time - Match Clocks
Time - What Time Will It Be?

# How Long Did It Take Worksheet

1. Suppose you gave the mouse the cookie at 11:00 a.m. and he promised to sweep the house. Two hours later the mouse had finished sweeping the whole house. What time would it be when he finished? Draw the hands on the clock and then write your answer below.

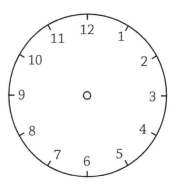

2. The mouse was tired and decided to take a nap. When the mouse finished his nap it was 3:20 p.m. Can you draw the arrows on the clock for 3:20?

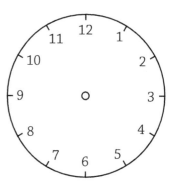

3. The following clock shows the time the mouse asked for a glass of cold milk. What time does it read?

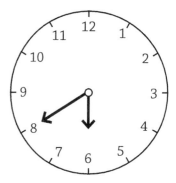

4. It was 7:05 when the mouse's mother came to pick him up at the end of your play date. Show that time on both the analog clock and the digital clock.

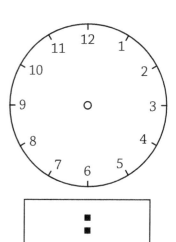

# Activity 5: Milk and Cookies

### PART 1

Before the lesson, empty a two-liter bottle and fill a half-gallon milk or juice container with water.

Tell students that they are going to give some milk to the mouse. Show the students the two-liter bottle and the half-gallon container and ask them which they think holds more liquid. "Which would the mouse rather have?"

Pour the water from the half-gallon container into the two-liter bottle. It should not quite fill the two-liter bottle. The actual equivalence is 1 gallon = 3.79 liters, so $\frac{1}{2}$ gallon is approximately 1.90 liters.

You may also want to use a 1-liter bottle and a quart size container to show that the 1-liter bottle holds slightly more than the quart container. The conversion is 1 quart = 0.95 liters.

Explain to students that when we use the terms half-gallons or liters, we are describing the measure of the **volume** of the containers. Because the volume of the liter is greater than the volume of the half-gallon, the mouse would rather have a liter of milk.

### PART 2

For any activities measuring weight, you will need access to a small digital scale that can measure grams. An alternative to the digital scale is a plastic scale and gram unit blocks.

If school policies allow it, bring in several different types of cookies. Ask students to predict which cookie weighs the most. You may want to make a graph of the prediction using picture graphs or bar graphs. You might have students use their hands to weigh the cookies and then vote again for which cookie they think is the heaviest.

Now have students actually weigh the cookies and graph the results in a bar graph.

If school policy does not allow cookies in the classroom, you can measure healthier food items.

### PART 3

Have students complete the following worksheet.

# Milk and Cookies Worksheet

1. Suppose you worked at a farm that bottles milk. You keep all the milk in a large vat before it is put into containers. Below is a drawing of one of the huge vats you use. Each mark represents 120 liters of milk. If this vat is filled to the top line, how much milk is in the vat?

2. Your class has decided to bake a giant cookie. The entire cookie weighs 48 kilograms! To make it easier to move, you break it into 4 equal pieces. How heavy is each piece? Explain how you found your answer.

3. If one store bought cookie weighs 30 grams, how much will a bag of 20 cookies weigh? Explain how you found your answer.

CHAPTER 5: Activities based on

# LIBRARY LION

by Michelle Knudsen

**2.MD.10**
Draw a picture graph and a bar graph
(with single-unit scale) to represent
a data set with up to four categories.
Solve simple put-together, take-
apart, and compare problems using
information presented in a bar graph.

# Activity 1: Our Favorite Books

Read the story to the students. In this activity you will take a poll
in class about students' favorite type of books. Establish four
distinct categories of books by asking for ideas from students or
by choosing your own categories. A librarian might suggest the
books students in your class most enjoy.

Examples of categories include books about animals, books about
families, books about make-believe, etc.

As you poll the students about their favorites, keep a tally chart on
the board to record responses.

Next, either have students fill in the chart provided following
this activity or use the technology you commonly use in your
classroom.

If you use the provided chart, students can either create bar
graphs or picture graphs. To create picture graphs, create small
pictures of the categories for students to glue onto the graph.

**Using Technology**
One form of technology is Microsoft Excel. You would type your
data into a worksheet.

You would then **Insert** a **Column Chart** (note: Excel calls bar
charts column charts). It should look like the example on the left
after you delete the legend.

| Books about: | Number of students: |
|---|---|
| Animals | 8 |
| People | 5 |
| Make-Believe | 9 |
|  |  |

Another form of technology to use is a virtual grapher. The
National Library of Virtual Manipulatives has one. If you go to:
**nlvm.usu.edu** and click on **Data Analysis,** the first choice is a **bar
graph**. This graph is very easy to use with young children.

Once the graph is displayed you can ask questions such as:
"Which choice was most popular?"
"Which choice was least popular?"
"How many more children liked ___ than ___?"
"How many votes did ___ and ____ get together?"

# Favorite Books Chart Template

## Our Favorite Books

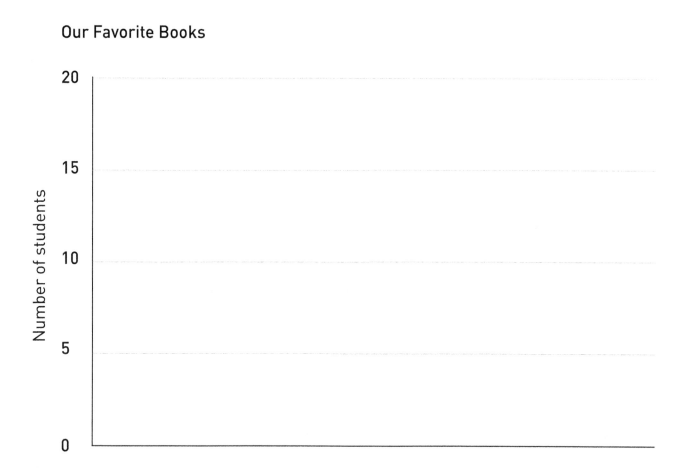

Favorite Books or Book Types

## Activity 2: Arranging Books

Have students study the following arrangement of books that Miss
Merriweather has made and write an equation to find the total
number of books she has used.

Example:

Students should have written one of the following equations:

2 books + 2 books + 2 books = 6 books
or
3 books + 3 books = 6 books

Explain that either equation is correct, but point out that both
equations result in the same answer of 6 books.

After answering any questions they may have about the equations,
ask them to complete the following worksheet.

# Counting Books in the Library Worksheet

1. How many total books has Mrs. Merriweather arranged in this section of the library? Be sure to write an equation as you did in the example. Also, explain how you found your answer.

2. How many total books were arranged in this section? Be sure to write an equation following the example. Explain how you found your answer.

3. Create your own drawing and write an equation to represent how many books there are.

## Activity 3: Story Time

Start with the following problem:

Imagine it was 12:15 when the lion arrived at the library. Miss Merriweather told him that story time was not until 3:00 p.m. How long did he have to wait for story time to begin?

After students have been given time to work on the problem, have them share answers and strategies. If no one has used a number line diagram to solve the problem, show them how they can:

Hours

Minutes

Have students do the following activities.

For further exploration or as a model, visit the National Library of Virtual Manipulatives:

**www.nlvm.usu.edu**

and click on Measurement (Grades 3-5). There are three TIME manipulatives:

Time - Analog and Digital Clocks
Time - Match Clocks
Time - What Time Will It Be?

# Story Time Worksheet

1. On Monday, the lion spent 50 minutes helping Miss Merriweather. On Tuesday, he spent another 35 minutes helping. How long did the lion spend helping Miss Merriweather for the two days combined? Explain how you found your answer.

2. On Wednesday, Story Time began a little early—at 2:50. If it lasted 1 hour and 25 minutes, what time did it finish? Use a number line to find the answer.

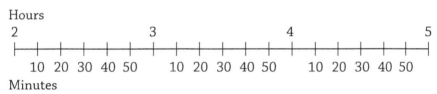

3. When the lion left the library on Thursday it was 6:05 p.m. If he had arrived at 11:35 a.m., how much time did he spend at the library?

4. When Miss Merriweather arrived on Friday she noticed that someone had taken all the numbers off the clock. Can you guess what time it was? Explain how you found your answer.

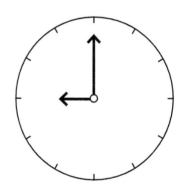

**3.OA.9**
Identify arithmetic patterns (including patterns in the addition table or multiplication table), and explain them using properties of operations. *For example, observe that 4 times a number is always even, and explain why 4 times a number can be decomposed into two equal addends.*

## Activity 4: Finding Patterns in Library Rules

After reading the book, tell students that in the library there are many rules to follow.

Every time someone takes one number into the library, they leave with a different number; but the rule to find the new number changes every day.

In this activity they must first discover the pattern and then figure out the rule that is used to create the new number.

**Example**
On Monday, when someone brings 1 into the library it changes to 4. If someone brings in a 2, it becomes a 5. A 3 will become a 6.

The numbers in the first column represent the numbers being taken into the library on Monday, and the numbers in the second column represent the numbers coming out. Fill in the rest of the table and find the rule that changes the number. Remember that the rule tells us what we must do to the number going in to find the number that comes out.

| IN | OUT |
|----|-----|
| 1 | 4 |
| 2 | 5 |
| 3 | 6 |
| 4 | 7 |
| 5 | 8 |
| 6 | 9 |

RULE: Add 3

# Library Rules Worksheet

For each day, determine the pattern, complete the table, and then write the rule.

### 1. Tuesday

| IN | OUT |
|----|-----|
| 1  | 6   |
| 2  | 7   |
| 3  | 8   |
| 4  |     |
| 5  |     |
| 6  |     |

RULE: _____

### 2. Wednesday

| IN | OUT |
|----|-----|
| 1  | 4   |
| 2  | 8   |
| 3  | 12  |
| 4  |     |
| 5  |     |
| 6  |     |

RULE: _____

### 3. Thursday

| IN | OUT |
|----|-----|
| 10 | 4   |
| 11 | 5   |
| 12 | 6   |
| 13 |     |
| 14 |     |
| 15 |     |

RULE: _____

### 4. Now make up your own rule for Friday. Complete the IN and OUT columns and write the rule.

| IN | OUT |
|----|-----|
|    |     |
|    |     |
|    |     |
|    |     |
|    |     |
|    |     |

RULE: _____

**3.OA.8**
Solve two-step word problems using the four operations. Represent these problems using equations with a letter standing for the unknown quantity. Assess the reasonableness of answers using mental computation and estimation strategies including rounding.

## Activity 5: Book Fines

Show students the following problem:
Each day that a book is late, the library charges a 5¢ fine. In addition, they charge a one time 50¢ processing fee for each book that is late. If your bill was 80¢, how many days late did you return the book?

Once students have examined the problem, ask them what they are trying to find. They should recognize that they must find the number of 'days' the book is late.

Tell them that because we don't know the number of days, it is the 'unknown' and we will call it **D**.

Now make a chart so students can start to see what is happening to the number of days or 'D'. Initially, just fill in Days and Fine. Leave the third column blank.

| Number of Days (D) | Fine (5¢ a day) | Total Bill (fine + processing fee) |
|---|---|---|
| 1 | 5¢ | 5¢ + 50¢ |
| 2 | 10¢ | 10¢ + 50¢ |
| 3 | 15¢ | 15¢ + 50¢ |
| 4 | | |
| 5 | | |

You want students to see that the fine is going up 5¢ every day.

You may also want to write 5 x1 next to the 5¢ and 5 x 2 next to the 10¢ etc., so students eventually see that you are multiplying the daily fine by number of days to determine the total fine.

Now ask the class, "If the book is 4 days late how much would you owe the library for just the fine?" They should find the answer using some form of following equation: 5¢ per day x 4 days = 20¢.

Now go back to the table and fill in the total fine amount column.

| Number of Days (D) | Fine (5¢ a day) | Total Bill (fine + processing fee) |
|---|---|---|
| 1 | 5¢ | 5¢ + 50¢ = 55¢ |
| 2 | 10¢ | 10¢ + 50¢ = 60¢ |
| 3 | 15¢ | 15¢ + 50¢ = 65¢ |
| 4 | 20¢ | 20¢ + 50¢ = 70¢ |
| 5 | 25¢ | 25¢ + 50¢ = 75¢ |

Summarize by explaining that, to find the total bill for any day, we should multiply the number of 'days' by 5¢ per day and then add the 50¢ processing fee.
So, we can write the equation: (4 days x 5¢ per day) + 50¢ = 70¢

In the problem they were given, they were told that the total bill was 80¢.
They can set up the equation: (D days x 5¢ per day) + 50¢ = 80¢

Explain that this is called a two-step equation and that our first step is to eliminate the number which is added to both sides of the equation. In this case, that number is 50¢.
If we subtract 50¢ (the processing fee) from both sides of the equation,
(D days x 5¢ per day) + 50¢ - 50¢ = 80¢ - 50¢
we have the equation: D days x 5¢ per day = 30¢

Now ask students what number when multiplied by 5 will equal 30. Allow them to determine their answer in any way they can. When they find the answer is 6, explain that D must equal six. The answer is 6 days.

**The students can practice with the following problem:**
Miss Merriweather decided to pay the lion for all his help at the library. She decided to give him $2 for every hour that he worked and then give him an extra bonus of $10. If the lion earned $34, how many hours did he work?

Once students have examined the problem, ask them what they are trying to find. They should recognize that they must find the number of hours the lion worked and this will be similar to finding the 'days' the book is late in the first problem.

Tell them that because we don't know the number of hours, it is the 'unknown'. Ask what letter they might use to represent it hours. They should choose H.

At this point you may use a chart similar to the chart used to determine the fine in the first example.

Guide them to the equation: (H hours worked x $2 per hour) + $10 = $34
Again, work through the solution.

This storyline can be used to create many problems of this type so that students become familiar with the model. **Some examples might be:**

7 books have already been donated to the library book drive and 3 more books are donated every day. How many days will it take for the book drive to achieve its goal of 40 books?

Also, change the problem by solving for other variables:
The lion loved reading a certain book (choose a class favorite). When he returned it to the library, his fine was 95¢. How many days late was the book? Revisiting the chart may help students write the equation.

CHAPTER 6: Activities based on

# OH, THE THINKS YOU CAN THINK!

by Dr. Seuss

## K.OA.1
Represent addition and subtraction with objects, fingers, mental images, drawings, sounds (e.g., claps), acting out situations, verbal explanations, expressions, or equations.

## K.OA.2
Solve addition and subtraction word problems, and add and subtract within 10, e.g., by using objects or drawings to represent the problem.

## K.OA.3
Decompose numbers less than or equal to 10 into pairs in more than one way, e.g., by using objects or drawings, and record each decomposition by a drawing or equation (e.g., 5 = 2 + 3 and 5 = 4 + 1).

## K.OA.4
For any number from 1 to 9, find the number that makes 10 when added to the given number, e.g., by using objects or drawings, and record the answer with a drawing or equation.

# Activity 1: The Rink-Rinker-Fink's Teeth

**PART 1**

In the book, we are asked if they "would dare yank a tooth of the Rink-Rinker-Fink?" Judging by the picture, the Rink-Rinker-Fink has 6 teeth.

Ask students if you were able to yank one tooth, how many would the Rink Rinker still have? Let them use any necessary means to come up with the answer of 5.

Write on the board that 1 + 5 = 6.

Now ask them if you were able to yank two teeth, how many would be left. Again, write 2 + 4 = 6

Continue the process for 3 through 5.

Depending on the ability of the class you may also want to ask if they pulled all the teeth, how many would remain. This leads to the equation 6 + 0 = 6

Explain to students that there are different ways to break up a number.

**PART 2**

For this activity, you may rather have students work collaboratively. Suppose that the Rink-Rinker-Fink has 8 teeth. Each student or group of students will examine a different equation. For example you can tell the first group they are pulling out 1 tooth, the second group 2 teeth, etc.

Use following Separating Teeth Template to give to the students as they remove or add teeth, or use another manipulative to represent the teeth (e. g. pattern block triangles would work well).

Students should complete the attached worksheet. Have them either place the "teeth" on the worksheet or actually glue them on. When all the students have finished, have a class discussion of the different ways to get 8.

# Separating Teeth Template

## Separating Teeth Worksheet

Imagine the Rink-Rinker-Fink has 8 teeth.

You are going to pull out _____.

Now he will still have_____ in his mouth.

Tooth Equation:  _____ + _____ = 8

**K.OA.1**

Represent addition and subtraction with objects, fingers, mental images, drawings, sounds (e.g., claps), acting out situations, verbal explanations, expressions, or equations.

**K.OA.2**

Solve addition and subtraction word problems, and add and subtract within 10, e.g., by using objects or drawings to represent the problem.

**K.OA.3**

Decompose numbers less than or equal to 10 into pairs in more than one way, e.g., by using objects or drawings, and record each decomposition by a drawing or equation (e.g., 5 = 2 + 3 and 5 = 4 + 1).

**K.OA.4**

For any number from 1 to 9, find the number that makes 10 when added to the given number, e.g., by using objects or drawings, and record the answer with a drawing or equation.

# Activity 2: The Rink-Rinker-Fink's Teeth continued

### PART 3

Now, tell students to suppose the Rink-Rinker-Fink had 10 teeth.

Use ten-frames to practice the counting strategy of "making 10". Again, you can use manipulatives or cut-out teeth using the template for the students to place in the ten-frame.

Give each student or group of students a different number of "teeth". Have them place the teeth in the ten-frame and count the number of teeth they will need to make ten.

When they complete the task, students should share their results. You may want to also demonstrate the way they can model each of the different situations using their fingers.

# Rink-Rinker-Fink's Ten-Frame Template

# Activity 3: Tallying Tails

## PART 1
This activity involves reading information from a graph and creating a graph given a table of values.

In the book, one of the questions asked is "How long is the tail of a zong?" In this activity, we examine the tail lengths of animals in our world. Keep in mind that not every lion has exactly the same size tail. In the same way people are different, animals differ, too, so the numbers are averages.

## PART 2
Explain to students that a raccoon's tail is about half as long as its entire body. If a student is 4 feet tall, how long would their tail would be?

### EXTENSIONS
An excellent connection is the book "If You Hopped Like a Frog" by David Schwartz. This book exemplifies feats children would be able to accomplish if they possessed animal characteristics. Multiplication is a natural extension of this book.

This is also a natural place to integrate science into mathematics class and discuss attributes of different animals. One activity might be to discuss the way different animals' eyes have adapted to their environment. For example, you might discuss frogs: their eyes are on top of their heads and they see only in front or above because threats to frogs rarely come from underneath. To simulate seeing like a frog, have students place plastic mirrors in front of their noses. This will allow them to see only straight ahead and above.

# Tallying Tails Worksheet 1

Below is a graph showing the lengths of the tails of 5 different animals. Use the graph to answer the questions. All lengths are in centimeters.

**Animal Tails**

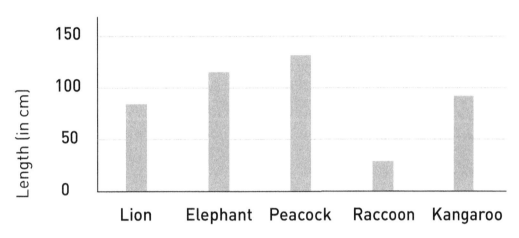

1. Which animal has the longest tail? ABOUT how long is it?

2. ABOUT how much longer is the kangaroo's tail than the raccoon's tail?

3. ABOUT how many raccoon's tails would you need to put together to be as long as one elephant's tail? Explain how you found your answer.

# Tallying Tails Worksheet 2

The last graph displayed animals' tails in centimeters. We are more used to seeing lengths in inches and feet. The following table of values shows the same lengths in inches. Use the information to construct a bar graph.

| Animal | Tail Length (in inches) |
|---|---|
| Lion | 33 |
| Elephant | 48 |
| Peacock | 54 |
| Raccoon | 11 |
| Kangaroo | 35 |

## Animal Tails

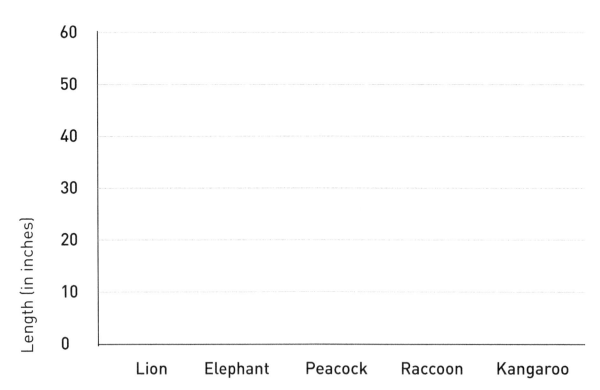

# TEACHER'S NOTES

**2.NBT.1**
Understand that the three digits of a three-digit number represent amounts of hundreds, tens, and ones; e.g., 706 equals 7 hundreds, 0 tens, and 6 ones. Understand the following as special cases:
- 100 can be thought of as a bundle of ten tens — called a "hundred."
- The numbers 100, 200, 300, 400, 500, 600, 700, 800, 900 refer to one, two, three, four, five, six, seven, eight, or nine hundreds (and 0 tens and 0 ones).

**2.NBT.2**
Count within 1000; skip-count by 5s, 10s, and 100s.

**2.NBT.3**
Read and write numbers to 1000 using base-ten numerals, number names, and expanded form.

**2.NBT.4**
Compare two three-digit numbers based on meanings of the hundreds, tens, and ones digits, using >, =, and < symbols to record the results of comparisons.

**2.NBT.5**
Fluently add and subtract within 100 using strategies based on place value, properties of operations, and/or the relationship between addition and subtraction.

**2.NBT.7**
Add and subtract within 1000, using concrete models or drawings and strategies based on place value, properties of operations, and/or the relationship between addition and subtraction; relate the strategy to a written method. Understand that in adding or subtracting three-digit numbers, one adds or subtracts hundreds and hundreds, tens and tens, ones and ones; and sometimes it is necessary to compose or decompose tens or hundreds.

**2.NBT.8**
Mentally add 10 or 100 to a given number 100–900, and mentally subtract 10 or 100 from a given number 100–900.

# Activity 4: The Guff and Snuv Party

## PART 1

After reading the book, ask students if they remember how many circles the Guff has on its tail. As a class, count the circles. Now ask them if they could figure out how many circles 10 Guffs would have.

Strategies might include counting out or drawing 10 pictures.

Ask if they can skip count to find the answer. Lead the class in skip counting by 5's and keep track of how many times they skip count. Have the whole class skip count together by yelling out "5, 10, 15 ... 50".

Ask the students to find out the number of circles on the tails of 17 Guffs. Then ask about the tails of 24 Guffs. Skip count to find each number. Continue until a pattern is found.

Now ask students if they remember how many fingers each Snuv has. They have 10 fingers just like us. Ask them to skip count to figure out how many fingers 8 Snuvs would have. Continue with 15 and 21 Snuvs.

## PART 2

Now explain to students that there were a lot of Snuvs practicing dancing before the big dance. Suppose they counted all the Snuv fingers and found there were 450 fingers. What does the 4 tell us? What does the 5 tell us? What does the 0 tell us?

You may want to use Base-10 blocks to discuss place value with the students; Base-10 blocks are an excellent manipulative for this concept. In Base-10 blocks you would have 4 hundreds or 4 flats, 5 tens or longs, and 0 ones. This is also a time to informally discuss the difference between face value and place value. In the number 450, the first digit is a 4. The value of 4 refers to its FACE VALUE as a digit. Because it is in the hundreds position, or the third place from the right, its PLACE VALUE within the number is 400.

Now ask students what would happen if one more Snuv came to practice. How many more fingers would that be?

It would be 10 more fingers. How would that change our number? We now would have 460 Snuv fingers. This can again be illustrated with the Base-10 blocks by simply adding another ten or long.

Ask students how many fingers we would have to add if yet another Snuv came. They should soon see the pattern and recognize how easy it is to add 10 to a number.

Now present the following scenario: The next day when the Snuvs were practicing, there were a total of 610 fingers. If one Snuv had to leave, how many fingers would remain? They should be able to mentally subtract 10 from 610 to get 600. Repeat the question, asking what would happen if another Snuv left. Again, they should be able mentally take the 10 away to get 590.

After discussing this, you might want to model the problem using Base-10 blocks. 600 would simply be 6 flats (or hundreds). Remind students that they want to take 10 away; how do they do this when they don't have any tens, just hundreds. Eventually students should recognize that they must decompose one of the hundreds – that is exchange it for 10 tens or 10 longs. This notion of decomposition is vital if students are to understand how to use our standard subtraction algorithm. Once they have "traded" a flat (or 100) for 10 longs (or 10 tens), they can take one of the tens away, leaving 5 flats (5 hundreds) and 9 longs (9 tens) or 590.

Technology can also be used to illustrate decomposition using the NLVM "Base-10 Blocks" virtual manipulative. **www.nlvm.usu.edu**

## PART 3
Explain to students that today is the day of the big party for Guffs and Snuvs. At the party, there are 389 Guffs and 413 Snuvs.

Ask if there are more Guffs or more Snuvs?

Some students might say there are more Guffs because of the larger digits in the ones and tens positions. Students should understand that they must look at the largest position (or the digit in the first place to the left) first. In this case, we must look at the hundreds place first. Because the digit in that position is a 4 for Snuvs and only a 3 for Guffs, there are more Snuvs at the party.

Now ask students to determine how many Guffs and Snuvs there are altogether at the party. Allow them to use any method, but have them explain their methods. You may also want to show them how we can determine this using Base-10 blocks.

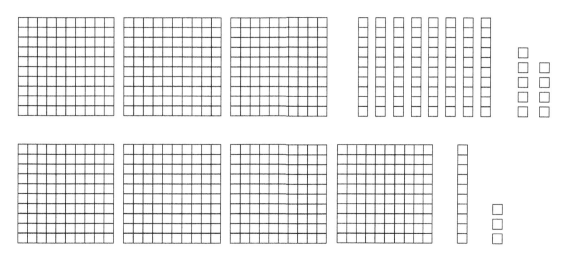

# Activity 5: The Bloog Games

### PART 1

Ask students if they can remember what Bloogs look like. Tell them that today we are going to imagine the Bloogs gathering for some games and then a feast.

The first game they are going to play is called Bloog Ball Bounce. Explain that even though Bloogs don't have hands, they can play by bouncing the ball off their heads back and forth to each other.

Now tell them that there are 12 Bloogs that want to play. Ask if every Bloog will be able to pair with a partner. When a student suggests that they can make pairs, ask them to demonstrate using 12 students. You might also want to use a magnetic manipulative (magnetic tape is a nice resource) and "stick" the Bloogs to a magnetic board.

Explain to the class that because each Bloog is able to pair with another Bloog with none leftover, 12 is an **even** number. When they pair but have one leftover, then they have an **odd** number.

Now, tell them that there are 15 Bloogs that want to play. Ask if 15 is an even or odd number. That is, can the Bloogs pair evenly or will there be one left over?

As a final example, use 19 Bloogs. Have all students write their answer and justify it using both a written explanation and a figure or drawing.

## PART 2

Now, explain that the Bloogs are sitting down for a feast after the games. Tell students that the Bloogs are sitting in 4 rows and in each row there are 2 seats.

Ask them to make a drawing that represents 4 rows with 2 seats in each row. Students should draw something similar to the figure below. They do not need to draw tables and chairs; they can simply draw rectangles to represent the seats.

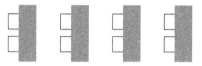

You may find that some students have drawn 2 rows with 4 seats in each, as shown in the example below. You should point out that the first example is the correct representation.

Take the first figure and ask students to write an addition equation to represent the seating. Help students see that we can think of this as: 2 + 2 + 2 + 2 = 8

You can do the same for second representation: 4 + 4 = 8

To informally assess, tell students to draw 5 rows with 3 seats in each row. Have students construct an addition equation to represent this new situation.

## PART 3

As a final activity, show them the following rectangular array and ask them to construct two addition equations to represent the total number of squares. The two equations are 4 + 4 + 4 = 12 and 3 + 3 + 3 + 3 = 12. Have the students explain their reasoning.

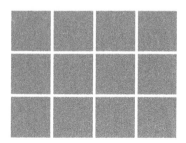

**3.OA.5**
Apply properties of operations as
strategies to multiply and divide.
*Examples: If 6 × 4 = 24 is known, then
4 × 6 = 24 is also known. (Commutative
property of multiplication.) 3 × 5 × 2
can be found by 3 × 5 = 15, then 15 × 2
= 30, or by 5 × 2 = 10, then 3 × 10 = 30.
(Associative property of multiplication.)
Knowing that 8 × 5 = 40 and 8 × 2 = 16,
one can find 8 × 7 as 8 × (5 + 2) = (8 × 5)
+ (8 × 2) = 40 + 16 = 56. (Distributive
property.)*

# Activity 6: Properties of Thinking

**PART 1**
Start with the following Think-Pair-Share problem:
The Royal chefs are cooking Schlopps. Each chef can make 6 Schlopps in one minute. On each Schlopp the chefs make, there are 4 cherries. If there are 3 chefs making Schlopps, how many cherries will they use in one minute?

Ask students to first think about the problem individually. After a few minutes, have them pair up to discuss their thoughts. Finally, have the whole class share their answer.

Students should see that they must multiply 6 x 4 x 3 (in any order) to get the final answer of 72.

Write 6 x 4 x 3 on the board. Divide the class in two. Explain to half of the class that they are going to first multiply the 6 by the 4. Draw parentheses around the 6 x 4 to emphasize they are doing that multiplication first. Then, they are going to take that product and multiply by 3. They should all get 72 again as an answer.

Explain to the other half of the class that they should multiply the 4 by the 3 first. Draw parentheses around the 4 x 3. They should take that product and multiply it by 6. They, too, should get 72.

Ask for students to share their thoughts after seeing this. In third grade, they do not need to know that this property is called the Associative Property of Multiplication. However, you certainly can share the term with them.

Ask if they can think of a situation in which it might be helpful to multiply the second two factors first. Show them this example: 43 x 5 x 2.

If we multiply the first two, we have 43 x 5, which certainly is not an easy multiplication to do. However, if we start with 5 x 2, we have 10. Now it is much easier to multiply 43 by 10 to get 430.

When we are adding, 5+7 gives us the same answer as 7+5. Is that true for multiplication as well? Have them think of an example to help prove or disprove this. Again, you can explain that the name of this property is the Commutative Property of Multiplication if you wish.

## PART 2

For this second activity, again divide the class into two groups. Tell students that the Royal chefs are again cooking Schlopps. On each Schlopp the chefs make, there are 4 sweet cherries and 3 sour cherries. If 5 chefs each make 1 Schlopp, how many cherries will they use?

Give half the class the expression: 5 (4 + 3). Give the other half the expression (5 x 4) + (5 x 3). You may have to remind students that order of operations require us to do the work inside a parentheses (4 + 3) first and that the order of operation is that multiplication is done before addition.

Treat this problem as a Think-Pair-Share. Ask each half of the class to share their findings.

This is the Distributive Property. In effect, we are distributing the 5 over the 4 and the 3 that are inside the parentheses.


## PART 3

As a review or an informal assessment, give students the following two problems and ask them to explain their reasoning.

1. In the book, they were having races with children on horses. The horses were on balls and the children had fish on their heads. Imagine a new race where 3 children sat on each horse and each child had two fish on their heads. If there were 9 horses in the race, how many total fish were there? Find two different ways to solve the problem.

2. The Rink-Rinker-Fink has three top teeth and three bottom teeth. If there are 8 Rink-Rinker-Finks, how many teeth are there altogether? We can solve this two ways. One way is to find out what 8(3 + 3) equals. Find another way. Do you get the same answer?

CHAPTER 7: Activities based on

# PEZZETTINO

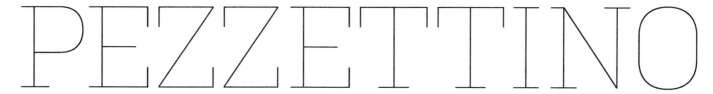

by Leo Lionni

# Activity 1: Creating Creatures from Squares and Triangles

Cut 1" x 1" (unit) squares out of blue, red, green, and yellow construction paper. You will need at least 12 of every color for each student or pair of students. (Using only 12 of each color limits the amount of counting. You can increase the difficulty for some students, offering more or less than 12 of each color.) You will also need poster paper or larger pieces of construction paper and glue.

## PART 1
After reading the book, give each student or pair of students the colored squares, a piece of poster paper, and glue.

Tell students that today they are creating their own creatures. You may want to have an example of one that you created to show the students. They should each create a name for their creature such as the-one-who-eats-pizza or the-sleeping-one.

Once they have decided on the shape they want to make, students glue the paper squares onto the poster paper to make their creatures. When they have finished gluing, you can either have them use inventive spelling to write the name of their creature on the poster board or an adult can write it for them.

After this has been completed, have them fill out the following worksheet to accompany their poster. You may want to check to see that they have counted correctly.

## PART 2
For this activity, you could have blue, red, green, and yellow unifix cubes available to students or use squares of colored paper.

After students have created their creatures and have completed the worksheet with their color counts, have them count out the proper number of unifix cubes of each color to reflect the number of squares in their creatures. For example, if the count of red squares in their creature was 11, they should count out 11 red unifix cubes. They should attach all the cubes of one color in a line and combine their lines with other classmates.

When everyone has completed the task, there should be one long, connected line of cubes (or a long line of paper squares) for each of the four colors.

Have the class count the squares in several different ways. Students could count the colored squares in each row or make groups of tens and count the tens and ones.

# Creature Worksheet

Our creature's name is: _____

Our creature has this many squares of each color:

Blue _____

Red _____

Green _____

Yellow _____

## Activity 2: Triangles and Squares

Using color tiles or squares and triangles cut from construction
paper, model a few of the character shapes in Pezzettino. Choose
an example of a character that has triangles and squares (e. g. one-
who-runs).

Make copies of the square and the two triangles on the next page to
demonstrate to students that two triangles can be put together to
form one square. If you have sets of tangrams available, you can use
the small triangles and square from the set for this demonstration.
(Note that there is a tangram template on page 14.)

Using multiple copies of the square template or the tangram
square, create the following shape for the students:

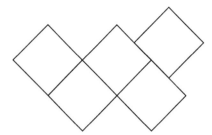

You should name this creature something that would be interesting
and/or relevant to your classroom.

Ask the students to count the number of squares in this creature
and then write '5' on the board.

Ask them to estimate how many triangles they think they would
have when they replace each of the squares with 2 triangles. Have
them replace the squares with triangles. Again, have them count.
They should now get 10. You can talk about the fact that there are
two triangles for every square, so the number of triangles is double
the number of squares.

5 + 5 = 10 is one of the doubling facts that students often learn
quickly.

Now create a larger shape using a greater number of squares and
again have them count the number of squares, replace them with
triangles, and count the number of triangles.

As an extension, have them create their own shapes out of different
numbers of squares and go through the counting, estimating,
replacing and recounting process.

# Pezzettino Shape Templates

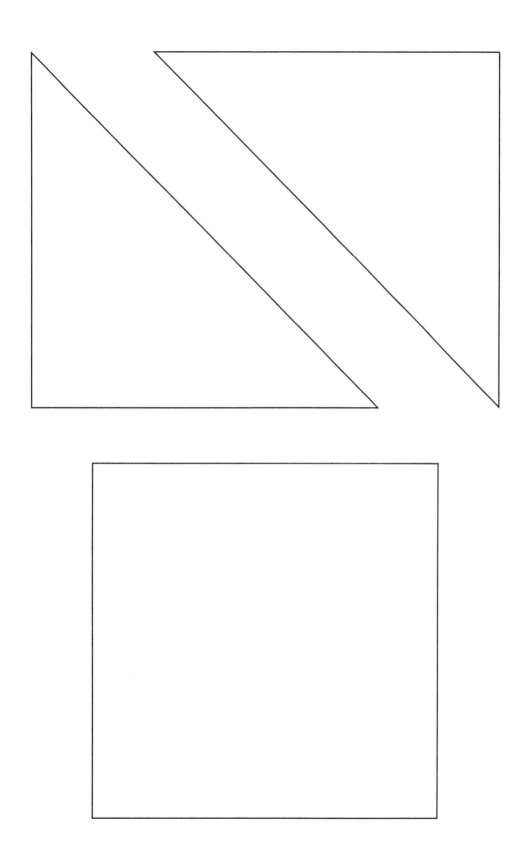

## Activity 3: How Many Shapes?

You may use color tiles or cut pieces from construction paper for this activity.

Read the story. Have the entire class look at the picture of the wise one and together count the number of blocks in the shape. There are 27 blocks in all.

Take 27 color tiles or pieces cut from construction paper and place them on a table.

Ask students to group the pieces into stacks of 10. They should have two stacks of 10 and seven left over.

Explain that the '2' in 27 refers to the 2 piles of 10 and the '7' refers to the seven ones left over.

Now have students work in groups. They will count the number of shapes used to create each of the characters in the book. When they count the number of pieces in a character, they should write the number in a table similar to **Figure 1**.

Next, have the students sort the number of shapes in each character into groups of 10 and any remaining ones and enter that information in a table similar to **Figure 2**.

Ask questions to reinforce their understanding:

Which shape has the greatest number of pieces? How many groups of ten are there in this shape?

Which shape has the least number of pieces? How many groups of ten are there in this shape?

Figure 1

| Character | Number of shapes |
|---|---|
| Pezzettino | |
| one-who-runs | |
| strong-one | |
| swimming-one | |
| one-on-the-mountain | |
| flying-one | |
| wise-one | |

Figure 2

| Character | Groups of 10 | Ones |
|---|---|---|
| Pezzettino | | |
| one-who-runs | | |
| strong-one | | |
| swimming-one | | |
| one-on-the-mountain | | |
| flying-one | | |
| wise-one | | |

## Activity 4: More or Less

First, using index sized cards or construction paper make a set of
cards that each have one of the following statements:
'< 12'; ' = 12'; or '> 12'.
Make enough cards so that each student has 1 card.

Have students randomly select one of the three cards and read
them as: "less than 12", "equal to 12", and "more than 12".

You may use color tiles or cut pieces from construction paper
for this activity. Students should take pre-cut construction paper
squares and/or triangles to represent the card they selected. For
example, if a student selected a card that read "more than 12", they
may choose to take any number of pieces more than 12. (You may
want to put an upper limit on the number of pieces they can use).
Students now make a character with their shapes. They should also
choose a silly name for their character such as one-that-hides-in-
trees.

After all the characters have been made, affix them to the board
arranged in the three groups.

Once the characters are arranged on the board, discuss each group.
E.g., for the "less than 12" group, count the number of shapes each
student used. Expect to see numbers such as 5, 8, 10, etc. Write
these numbers on the board and use the less than notation: 5 < 12;
9 < 12, etc. Do this for each of the three groups.

An extension would be to arrange the characters from the least
number of shapes to the greatest number of shapes. Select any two
shapes and use the 'less than' symbol to indicate the one that has
fewer pieces. You can then reverse the order and use the 'greater
than' symbol.

CHAPTER 8: Activities based on

# SOMEBODY LOVES YOU, MR. HATCH

by Eileen Spinelli

# Activity 1: The Shape of Cards

This lesson involves examining different shapes on cards. You may want to remind students that in the story Mr. Hatch received a little white card.

## PART 1

As a warm-up, give students paper and a ruler and ask them to create a card with a shape that has four sides, but isn't a rectangle. You may or may not choose to review the attributes of a rectangle first, reminding them that a square is a rectangle. Have students share their results and discuss why the shape they've made is not a rectangle.

## PART 2

Make a copy of the train card at the end of this activity. Ask students to name some of the shapes in the card.

Give students construction paper and tell them that they are going to create pictures for cards from shapes, too. The pictures they create will have the following criteria:
- They must use at least 5 shapes
- At least 3 of the shapes must be different
- 2 shapes must be put together to make a new shape
- They must write a poem in the card

## PART 3

For a final activity, have students draw a triangle on a sheet of paper. Give them rulers to draw straight lines. They can design the triangles in any way.

Remind them that any closed shape with 3 sides is a triangle. When they are drawn, display all the triangles and discuss which are similar and which are different.

The Train Card

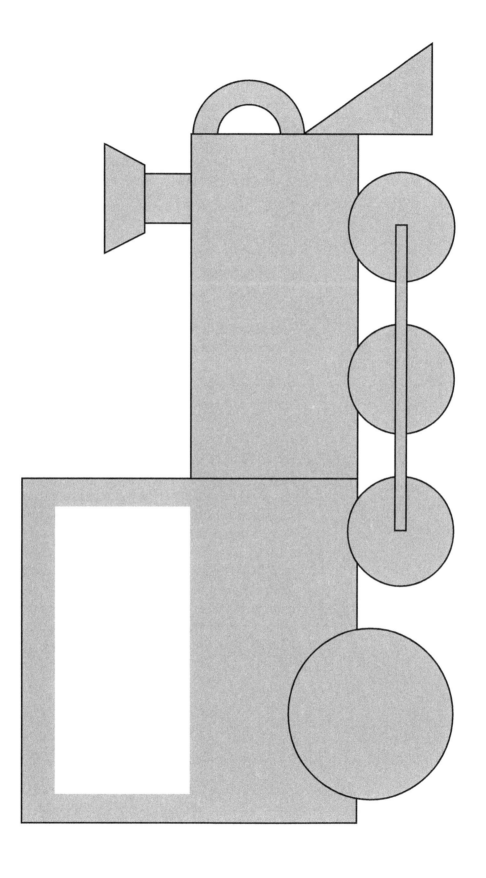

## Activity 2: The Price of Things

After reading the story, begin with this problem: On the way home from work, Mr. Hatch stopped at the newsstand to buy a paper. He used 2 quarters, 1 dime, and 1 nickel. How much did the newspaper cost?

Note: You may want to have students use plastic money or some other type of manipulative as they work through these money problems.

Now pose this problem: Mr. Hatch was so happy he baked brownies and made lemonade for everyone. Everyone loved the lemonade so much that the next day Tess and Tyrone decided to sell lemonade. They decided to charge 30¢ a glass.

Ask students to find two different ways to make 30¢. You can either have students use manipulatives or draw pictures of the coins.

Now challenge students with this extension: If Tess and Tyrone sold 5 glasses of lemonade, how much money would they have from the sales?

Have students discuss the strategies they used to determine the answer. As an example, some might choose to count out a quarter and a nickel for each of the 5 glasses sold. They would then combine the 4 quarters to make $1 and the extra quarter and 5 nickels to make another 50¢.

Now have students create their own word problems—either based on Mr. Hatch, a different story, or on a tale of their own. Have students share their stories. You may want to set up stations where students walk around and try to solve each other's problems after all have been first checked for accuracy.

## 2.OA.1

Use addition and subtraction within 100 to solve one- and two-step word problems involving situations of adding to, taking from, putting together, taking apart, and comparing, with unknowns in all positions, e.g., by using drawings and equations with a symbol for the unknown number to represent the problem.

## 2.OA.2

Fluently add and subtract within 20 using mental strategies. By end of Grade 2, know from memory all sums of two one-digit numbers.

## 2.OA.3

Determine whether a group of objects (up to 20) has an odd or even number of members, e.g., by pairing objects or counting them by 2s; write an equation to express an even number as a sum of two equal addends.

## Activity 3: Lots of Cards

After reading the story, tell students that Mr. Hatch has become so popular he receives many more cards.

Give students the following problem: Suppose that Mr. Hatch receives 4 cards on Monday and then 3 more cards each day of the week. How many cards will he have on Friday? Ask if students can compute the answer mentally. Ask for volunteers to explain how they would compute the answer.

Possible answers include starting with 4 and then simply skip counting by 3 after that. Another possible technique would be to add Tuesday through Friday or 3+3+3+3 to get 12 and then add 4 more to get 16.

Ask students if 16 is an even or odd number. Have a volunteer use color tiles or any other counters to show that every counter can be paired with another so 16 is even. Explain that one way to get 16 is to add 4+3+3+3+3.

Now present students with the following problem: Mr. Hatch wanted to write thank-you notes for all the kind cards he had received. He bought one package that had 18 cards in it and two more packages that each had 12 cards in them. How many total thank-you cards did he buy? Allow students to use any method they choose to solve this. Have students share some of their methods with the class.

The following worksheet provides practice and exploration for these concepts.

# Lots of Cards Worksheet

1. If Mr. Hatch received 8 regular cards and 7 that play music when you open them, how many cards did he receive? Explain how you could solve this mentally.

2. Mr. Hatch received so many cards that he had to move some cards to his garage for storage. Of the 19 cards he received last week, he moved 11 to his garage. How many cards did he not move to the garage? Explain how you could solve this mentally.

3. Is 19 an even number or an odd number? Pretend that Mr. Hatch did not know the difference between even and odd numbers. How would you explain to him which type of number 19 is?

4. Two weeks ago Mr. Hatch received 34 cards. Last week he received 19. If he receives 21 next week, how many cards would he have altogether?

5. Mr. Hatch bought 60 stamps at the post office for his holiday cards. If he used 18 of them, how many does he still have left? Explain how you got your answer.

## Activity 4: More Cards

After reading the story, tell students that Mr. Hatch has become so popular he receives many cards. Give students the following problem:

Mr. Hatch received 70 cards every week. How many cards will he have after 2 weeks? After 6 weeks? After 10 weeks?

After students have had time to think about the problem, explore different strategies for solving.

One way to keep track of all the data would be with the use of a table such as:

| Week | Number of Cards |
|------|-----------------|
| 1 | 70 |
| 2 | 140 |
| 3 | 210 |
| 4 | 280 |
| 5 | 350 |
| 6 | 420 |
| 7 | 490 |
| 8 | 560 |

Students may have different strategies for adding the 70 new cards every week. An excellent strategy for students to demonstrate place-value knowledge would be to keep adding another 7 to the tens column. That is, add 7+7 = 14 and then put zero in the units position to make 140; 14 + 7 = 21 which leads to 210.

Take advantage of this time to let students experiment with alternative algorithms or strategies that are different than the traditional two-column addition algorithm.

You may also want to use base ten blocks to reinforce addition. Students can model 70 + 70 by adding 7 longs (or tens) + 7 longs to get 14 longs. Now, they can trade in 10 of the longs for a flat (hundred), giving 1 flat and 4 longs or 100 + 40 or 140.

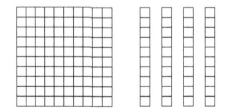

A second problem that deals with both addition and subtraction:

To show his appreciation for all the lovely cards, Mr. Hatch baked cookies to give to all his new friends. He baked 300 cookies. He gave 25 cookies to his friends each day. How many cookies will he have given away in 5 days? 10 days? How many cookies will Mr. Hatch have remaining on the 10th day?

For assessment, give students the following problem to check their understanding:
Mr. Hatch decided to count the cards the postman, Mr. Goober, delivered to him. He counted 246 cards in May and 197 cards in June.

a) How many cards did he get in both months, May and June?

b) How many more cards did he receive in May than in June?

c) If Mr. Hatch hoped to get 500 cards, how many would he need to receive in July to reach his goal?

Have students show all work and explain how they arrived at their answers.

# Activity 5: Mr. Hatch Likes the Number 10

**PART 1**

Present this problem: Mr. Hatch received lots of cards from his new friends. One card that he received had a picture of 10 flowers on it. If Mr. Hatch received 5 of these cards, how many flowers would he have received altogether? Show the method you used to find your answer.

Pose the same problem using different numbers of cards until children are comfortable with multiples of 10.

# Worksheet for Mr. Hatch Likes the Number 10, Part 1

1. Mr. Hatch ordered cards online. Each card had 7 shapes on it. If Mr. Hatch ordered 10 cards, how many total shapes were on the 10 cards?

2. Draw a picture of a card that has 7 shapes on it. Design it in any way you would like.

3. How could the card you drew help you to answer question #1?

4. Every night Mr. Hatch ate a fresh turkey wing for dinner. Imagine that he also ate 10 grapes. At the end of 9 days, how many grapes would he have eaten? Explain how you found your answer.

# Activity 5: Mr. Hatch Likes the Number 10 continued

**PART 2**
Rounding whole numbers.

Ask students to consider the following problem: Suppose that Mr. Hatch worked at the newsstand for Mr. Smith, and he sold 28 papers. If Mr. Smith asked Mr. Hatch for an estimate of how many papers he sold, which would be a closer estimate, 20 or 30?

Explain to students that when we round to the nearest ten, we must look at the digit in the one's place. If that digit is 5 or higher we round up to the next multiple of ten. If the digit is 4 or less, we round down.

One way to highlight the concept of rounding is to take a Hundreds Chart and have students use a highlighter to highlight the entire columns of 5's, 6's, 7's, 8's, and 9's. They should use that same color to make an arrow pointing to the right above the chart. This visual chart shows that if the number ends in a 5 or higher, they will round up to the next ten.

They could then highlight the 1's through 4's in a different color. Above these columns, draw an arrow pointing to the left. This shows that for a number ending in a 4 or lower they will round down.

Now give the students this problem: Mr. Hatch estimates that in the course of a year, he eats about 620 prunes. How can we round 620 to the nearest 100?

Because we are rounding to the nearest hundred, we look at the place immediately to the right of the hundreds place. That would be the tens place. Have them circle the 2. Remind them that because it is less than 4 our answer is 600.

Have students practice rounding up and down with the following worksheet.

# Worksheet for Mr. Hatch Likes the Number 10, Part 2

1. Mr. Hatch reads 7 newspapers every week. How would you round this number to the nearest 10?

2. There are 3 steps to the back porch of Mr. Hatch's house and 12 steps to the second floor. Mr. Hatch climbed the porch steps and then went to the second floor. When you round to the nearest 10, how many steps did he climb?

3. Mr. Hatch loves jelly beans. He has estimated that there are 20 jelly beans in a packet. What is the fewest number of jelly beans that a packet should hold? The greatest number?

4. Mr. Hatch's neighbor has about 275 daisies crowding her garden. If you round to the nearest 100, about how many daises does she have growing in her garden?

# Activity 6: Mr. Hatch Commutes

For this fun activity, set up either your classroom or a large area such as the gymnasium to represent Mr. Hatch's town.

Because we are told that his brick house is 8 blocks away from the shoelace factory where Mr. Hatch works, you will need to make a picture or a model of his house and put tape down on the floor to represent the city block grid.

On his way home from work, Mr. Hatch makes two stops: the newsstand; and the grocery store. Decide where the newsstand and grocery store could be or let students decide.

Once the "town" is set up, have students measure the distance from a) his house to the factory; b) the factory to the newsstand; c) the newsstand to the grocery store; and d) the grocery store back to his house.

All measurements should be to the nearest quarter of an inch.

After the measurements have been made, students could color on the following chart the number of blocks Mr. Hatch walks and compare the number of blocks to the distance they measured.

### Example
Mr. Hatch never uses short cuts through blocks. Suppose the doctor's office is 4 blocks walking distance away from Mr. Hatch's house. These are some of the places the doctor's office can be.

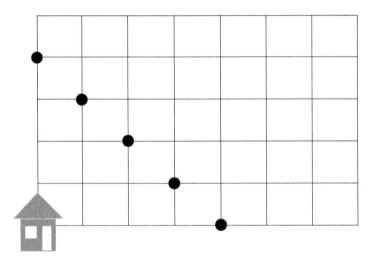

# Table Template

On this table, color in the number of blocks Mr. Hatch must walk when he travels from:

## Mr. Hatch's Travels

| Number of Blocks | 9 | | | | |
|---|---|---|---|---|---|
| | 8 | | | | |
| | 7 | | | | |
| | 6 | | | | |
| | 5 | | | | |
| | 4 | | | | |
| | 3 | | | | |
| | 2 | | | | |
| | 1 | | | | |
| | Number of Blocks | Home to Factory | Factory to News Stand | News Stand to Grocery Store | Grocery Store to Home |

When you have filled in the columns with different colors, you will have a bar graph of the distances.

CHAPTER 9: Activities based on

# THE VERY HUNGRY CATERPILLAR

by Eric Carle

# Activity 1: Creating Caterpillars

### PART 1
First, create a bag of shapes for each student. The bags should each contain 13, 15, 17 or 19 shapes, using odd numbers so that students are able to divide the shapes into two unequal piles. The shapes can be a combination of cutouts and any manipulatives that you have. A mix of materials would work well, such as some pattern blocks, some attribute shapes, some color tiles, some unifix cubes, etc. A mix of different colors and different shapes are important, too, and even might include three-dimensional objects; the only caveat is that all objects should be relatively the same size.

Tell students that they are going to make caterpillars with the objects in the bag you have given them.

Ask students to first separate the objects in the bag into 2 piles by using any attribute they choose. For example, they may choose a pile of shapes that have four sides and then a pile of manipulatives that have more or less than four sides. Or they may separate by color. You want to encourage them to be creative when choosing attributes. Once they have separated their shapes, ask them to count the number of objects they have in each pile. Finally, ask them to explain which pile has more and why.

### PART 2
Now have students put the two piles together and count out ten shapes. Have them put the pile of ten together and then count how many they have left over. Have different students report to the class that they have 'one pile of ten with _____ ones left over'. As students present their findings, write each equation on the board.

For example, if one student had the 15, she would explain "I had a pile of 10 with 5 ones left over". On the board write: 10 + 5 = 15

### PART 3
Now ask students to use their shapes to build a caterpillar. Decide beforehand whether they must use all the shapes in their bag or if they may choose which shapes they want to be a part of the caterpillar.

After students have finished, lead them on a gallery walk to view the caterpillars. Along the way, select various caterpillars and ask questions such as: What is similar about these two?; What is different?; How many sides does this shape have?; Does anyone know what we call this shape?; Which caterpillar is made of the largest number of shapes?

**K.CC.2**
Count forward beginning from a given number within the known sequence (instead of having to begin at 1).

**K.CC.7**
Compare two numbers between 1 and 10 presented as written numerals.

**K.OA.5**
Fluently add and subtract within 5.

## Activity 2: More or Less

After reading the book, give students a number of manipulatives such as unifix cubes or chips cut from construction paper.

Pose the following question: "On Wednesday, the caterpillar ate three plums and on Friday, he ate five oranges. Which number is larger, 3 or 5?"

Ask the same type of question repeatedly until students answer correctly every time.

Then, write the numbers 4 and 7 on the board and ask which number is larger. Ask students to back up their solutions by modeling with the manipulatives.

Now explain that on Saturday, the caterpillar ate a LOT. He started with one piece of chocolate cake. Then he ate an ice cream cone and a pickle. How many things did he eat? Ask a series of these questions involving simple addition and subtraction of food items.

Finally, to practice counting on, tell the students to imagine the caterpillar had already eaten four things. Using the Saturday scenario to practice, say "If he has already eaten 4 things, the cake will make 5, the ice cream 6, and the pickle 7." Students can practice beginning with different numbers and adding different food, counting on to 14 or more.

**1.NBT.1**

Count to 120, starting at any number less than 120. In this range, read and write numerals and represent a number of objects with a written numeral.

**1.NBT.4**

Add within 100, including adding a two-digit number and a one-digit number, and adding a two-digit number and a multiple of 10, using concrete models or drawings and strategies based on place value, properties of operations, and/or the relationship between addition and subtraction; relate the strategy to a written method and explain the reasoning used. Understand that in adding two-digit numbers, one adds tens and tens, ones and ones; and sometimes it is necessary to compose a ten.

**1.NBT.5**

Given a two-digit number, mentally find 10 more or 10 less than the number, without having to count; explain the reasoning used.

**1.NBT.6**

Subtract multiples of 10 in the range 10-90 from multiples of 10 in the range 10-90 (positive or zero differences), using concrete models or drawings and strategies based on place value, properties of operations, and/or the relationship between addition and subtraction; relate the strategy to a written method and explain the reasoning used.

# Activity 3: Lots of Leaves

Read the story. Pose the following problem: Suppose you were a biologist studying caterpillars and you discovered that, before going into a cocoon, one caterpillar had eaten 89 leaves.

Now point to the 8 and ask the students what the digit means or represents. They should all understand that the 8 refers to 8 sets of 10 or 80. Now point to the 9 and ask the same question. They should answer that it represents 9 ones. Remind them that 80 +9 = 89.

Now ask: How many more leaves would the caterpillar need to eat to get to 100? Ask students for a counting strategy to find the number. You do not want to use the subtraction algorithm, but instead, lead students to count up to 100. You may want to have cut-out paper leaves or other manipulatives available to stick to the board. The objective of this lesson is to practice counting on from a number—not the skill of subtraction.

Return to the number 89. Explain that another researcher found that you counted wrong and the number of leaves the caterpillar ate should have been 10 less. Ask students if they could find the new number without doing any written work. When they determine that the answer is 79, break the number into tens and ones to show. 79 = 70 + 9 or 7 tens + 9 ones.

Show them that when you take 10 away, you have one less ten and the same number of ones: 79. A Hundreds Chart is a good tool to allow students to see this relationship. If they want to add or subtract 10 they only need to move up or down a column on the chart. A number line displaying increments of ten is another simple tool to demonstrate adding and subtracting ten.

Now pose the following problem: Another caterpillar has already eaten 30 leaves. If he eats another 40 leaves, how many leaves would he have eaten altogether?

Talk about the different strategies students use to solve this problem. For instance, some may choose to think of it as 3 tens + 4 tens = 70 tens, or 70. Other students may look on the hundreds chart and move up four columns.

Now ask: If there were 80 leaves on one tree before the caterpillar started eating, and then 60 leaves after she finished, how many leaves did the caterpillar eat. Again, note the strategy used.

As a final question ask: "As a biologist researcher, you decided to count cocoons. You found 32 cocoons on one tree and 15 cocoons on another tree. How many cocoons did you find?"

Have students describe their strategies.

At this time, you may want to show them how to add the two numbers using base-10 blocks. Base-10 blocks are a wonderful tool for early place value understanding.

To model this problem, show them 32 as three tens and 2 ones and 15 as 1 ten and 5 ones. Now explain that we add the 3 tens and 1 ten to get 4 tens; we also add the 2 ones and 5 ones to get 7 ones. So, our final answer is 4 tens and 7 ones or 47.

For a review and assessment, have students work individually or cooperatively on the following three questions:

1. Dr. Cruz was a researcher who collected rare caterpillar species. She had 43 of one species and 36 of another. How many caterpillars did she have altogether?

2. At one time, Dr. Cruz had 97 leaf samples. If she gave10 away, how many would she have?

3. Dr. Cruz also collects the butterflies. She had 50 Monarch butterflies but gave 20 to a local elementary school. How many butterflies did she have left?

# Activity 4: Lots of Fruit

After reading the book, ask students to estimate how many pieces of fruit they think the caterpillar ate during the week.

Then, as you read the story again, help them to add the fruit to find the answer. You may want to have them model along with you using either cutout shapes as manipulatives or any counting device such as blocks or chips.

1 apple + 2 pears + 3 plums = 6 pieces of fruit.

Now, add the four strawberries:
6 pieces + 4 strawberries = 10 pieces of fruit.

Now, add the 5 oranges:
10 pieces + 5 oranges = 15 pieces of fruit.

Ask if they think they would get a stomach ache if they ate that much fruit.

Now ask this question: "What if there were a different caterpillar who ate 7 apples on one day. Then he had more apples on the second day. Altogether he ate 11 apples. How can we find out how many apples he ate on the second day?

On board, write $7 + ? = 11$.

Help students to model with hands-on, concrete resources. They should start with 7 apples or blocks, etc. Then they can count how many more they would need to add on until they got to 11. The process of adding on 4 more apples should be a powerful model for them.

If the idea needs reinforcement, you can pose more questions: "What if there were a different caterpillar who ate 7 apples on one day. Then he had even more apples on the second day. Altogether he ate 15 apples. How can we find out how many apples he ate on the second day?

Now try a similar situation involving subtraction: Another caterpillar, little Carli, had 9 oranges in a pile. She ate some of them and had only 6 left. How many oranges did she eat?

Ask the students if they could write an equation to represent that:
$9 - ? = 6$

Have them try to model the situation with the manipulatives. You may also want to have them try to explain how they determined how many oranges they had to take away.

Now suggest a situation in which they must add multiple items. Ask: Before Barry the Butterfly was a butterfly, he was a caterpillar that also needed to eat a lot of fruit. One day he ate 4 pears, 7 strawberries and 6 plums. How many pieces of fruit did he eat that day?

Have students try to model this with an equation and then use manipulatives to arrive at the answer: 4 + 7 + 6 = ?

**Worksheet extension** (you will need to make copies of the following worksheet):
Give each student (or groups of students if they are working collaboratively) 3 dice and ask them to complete the following worksheet. They should roll each die, write down the result, and select a food item to go with each number. For example, if they rolled a 3, 6, and 4, they might write 3 pieces of pizza, 6 candy bars, and 4 ice cream sundaes.

Then have students add the three numbers up to find the sum.

As a review, ask students to imagine you have 4 apples. Place four magnetic apples on the board or draw four apples. Now ask what happens if we add 3 more apples. Have the class count as you add first one apple (to get 5), a second apple (to get 6) and a third apple (to get the answer of 7). Ask someone to explain that addition is just like counting on. If they want to find the answer to 4 + 3 = ?, they could begin at 4 and count on another 3 to get 7.

Students who need practice can repeat this. Give them equations such as: 8 + 4 = ?
6 + 7 = ?

## Lots of Fruit Worksheet

**Roll each die.**

Write the number on the die:                Write the name of the food you chose:

1) _____                          _____

2) _____                          _____

3) _____                          _____

Add: Write the equation for line 1, plus line 2, plus line 3.

_____ + _____ + _____ = _____

**Roll each die again.**

Write the number on the die:                Write the name of the food you chose:

1) _____                          _____

2) _____                          _____

3) _____                          _____

Add: Write the equation for line 1, plus line 2, plus line 3.

_____ + _____ + _____ = _____

**Roll each die again.**

Write the number on the die:                Write the name of the food you chose:

1) _____                          _____

2) _____                          _____

3) _____                          _____

Add: Write the equation for line 1, plus line 2, plus line 3.

_____ + _____ + _____ = _____

# TEACHER'S NOTES

CHAPTER 10: Activities based on

# WHERE THE WILD THINGS ARE

by Maurice Sendak

**K.MD.2**

*Directly compare two objects with a measurable attribute in common, to see which object has "more of"/"less of" the attribute, and describe the difference. For example, directly compare the heights of two children and describe one child as taller/shorter.*

**K.MD.3**

*Classify objects into given categories; count the numbers of objects in each category and sort the categories by count.*

# Activity 1: Monster Attributes

Ask students to count all the characters in the book.

Now ask them to classify characters as either human or not human. Make a table on the board (or computer projector) to display the results. You can have students use tally marks as they count:

| Human | Not Human |
|-------|-----------|
|       |           |

Ask questions based on results such as: "Are there the same amount of people and characters who are not people?"; "Which group has more members?"

Ask students to classify monsters as having horns or not having horns. Again, make a table and ask probing questions.

| Horns | No Horns |
|-------|----------|
|       |          |

Now ask students to find different attributes that they would like to explore based on the book. These attributes can involve characters or pictures from the book, such as all things of a certain shape or a certain color. Have them construct a table and ask then ask questions based on the data they collect.

As an extension, have students count the number of letters in their name and make a class table based on the number of letters (E.g., Pete has 4, Lucinda has 7). Compare the results asking questions such as: Which name has the greatest number of letters? Which has the least? How many names have the same number of letters? Which number of letters has the most names?

# Monster Attributes Chart Templates

| Human | Not Human |
|---|---|
|  |  |

| Horns | No Horns |
|---|---|
|  |  |

2.G.1
Recognize and draw shapes having
specified attributes, such as a given
number of angles or a given number
of equal faces. Identify triangles,
quadrilaterals, pentagons, hexagons,
and cubes.

# Activity 2: Making Monsters

**PART 1**  2 Dimensions

Remind students that the monsters in the book all had distinctive features.

Explain that today they are going to create "monsters" with certain features.

Give each student or group of students one copy of the Making Monsters template sheet and ask them to create a monster with the following specifications. Note that they are allowed to use the same shape twice. They could trace the shapes onto another sheet of paper, or cut out the shapes and glue them onto a separate sheet. You should have additional sheets available.

Monster specifications:
- Their monster must contain at least 4 different shapes
- They cannot use more than a total of 6 different quadrilaterals
- They must use at least two shapes that do not have equal sides
- Their monster must have between 8 shapes and 16 shapes

When students complete the task, they can share their monsters with the class. You can use a peer review to make certain all the specifications have been met.

**PART 2**  3 Dimensions

If you have access to 3-dimensional blocks (i.e., cubes, cylinders, spheres, rectangular prisms, etc.) you can have students try this extension activity.

Students can again make monsters based on specific attributes using 3-D blocks to create the monsters.

Some specifications can be:
- The monster must have exactly 3 shapes with equal faces and 3 shapes with unequal faces.
- The monster must have at least two shapes that have at least one circular face.

# Making Monsters Template

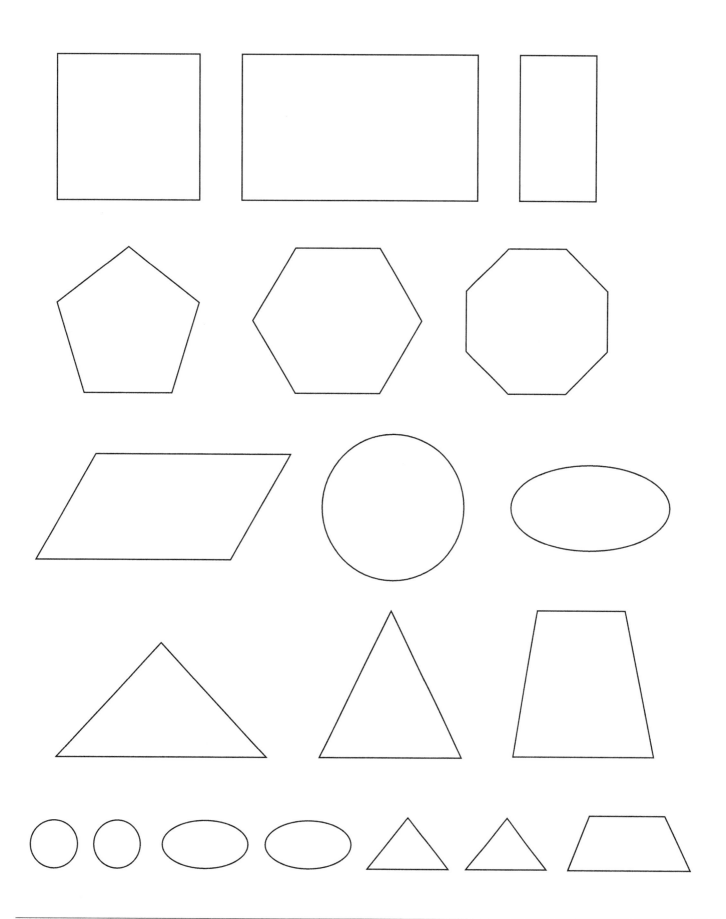

**2.MD.1**
Measure the length of an object by selecting and using appropriate tools such as rulers, yardsticks, meter sticks, and measuring tapes.

**2.MD.2**
Measure the length of an object twice, using length units of different lengths for the two measurements; describe how the two measurements relate to the size of the unit chosen.

**2.MD.3**
Estimate lengths using units of inches, feet, centimeters, and meters.

**2.MD.4**
Measure to determine how much longer one object is than another, expressing the length difference in terms of a standard length unit.

# Activity 3: Max's Boat

**PART I** Small Boats

Students are going to make boats out of various shapes. You can use any manipulative such as pattern blocks, color tiles, attribute shapes, tangrams, or shapes cut from colored paper. You also need rulers that measure the boats in both customary (inches) and metric (centimeters) units.

First ask the students: "If we were going to measure the width of our desks, would we want to use inches, feet, or miles?" Discuss why each option would or would not be chosen.

Now have students use the shapes you've chosen to create a boat either on their desks or on a sheet of paper. If they are tracing shapes, they can then color them in.

Ask them to begin to fill out the accompanying worksheet, writing an estimate for how long their boat is (at the longest point) in inches. Now ask them to measure the actual length of the boat and record the value. You can choose to have them measure to the nearest half inch or quarter inch. Check students' work here for errors. Each value should be between 5 and 20 inches.

Once they are comfortable with inches, repeat the procedure using the metric system.

Ask: "If we were using the metric system, would we use kilometers, meters, or centimeters?"

Now ask them to estimate the length of their boat in centimeters. Have them enter their estimate on the following worksheet and then measure the boat in centimeters. Ask students (or groups of students) if they see any relationship between the length in inches and the length in centimeters.

Now collect all their data (or just use one or two student's data) and double and triple the length of the boat in inches.

For example, if the length of the boat in inches was 9, write the length doubled (= 18) and the length tripled (= 27). This will reinforce addition skills and is included on the worksheet.

More importantly, because 1 inch is equal to 2.54 centimeters, the measurement in centimeters should fall about halfway between the two values of length in inches doubled and length in inches tripled. This is an important relationship and we should begin to reinforce this relationship of inches to centimeters.

**PART 2** Big Boats

You can follow the same procedure used in the small boats in Part 1, but
instead have students create large boats either on the classroom floor or in a hallway
or gymnasium.

You may want to use big blocks or to cut out large shapes for them to work with.

You may consider having the entire class work on the same boat. For measurement,
you would use feet and meters.

In this case, 1 meter is a little larger than 3 feet, so you don't need to double the value
to determine feet. Instead, just triple the length in feet.  The value for meters will be
a little greater.

You can also quadruple the length in feet and show that the value in meters is between
the feet tripled and feet quadrupled, again demonstrating the relationship between
the metric and customary system.

# Max's Boat Worksheet

Draw a picture of your boat:

1) Write your estimate for the length of your boat in inches. _____

2) Now measure your boat. How many inches long is it? _____

3) Now take your answer from question (2) and double it:

_____ inches long + _____ inches long  = _____ inches long

4) Now take your answer from question (2) and triple it:

_____ inches long + _____ inches long + _____ inches long = _____ inches long

5) Enter your estimate for the length of your boat in centimeters. _____

6) Now measure your boat using centimeters. How long is it? _____

7) What do you notice about the answer in centimeters (#6) and the answers in (#3) and (#4)?

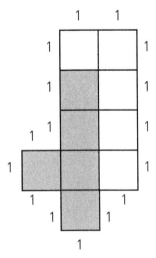

# Activity 4: Wild Thing Island

This activity involves students using pentominoes to create islands where the monsters can live.

Explain to students that the perimeter of a shape is the distance around the outside of it. Draw a square on the board and point to one of the sides. Tell them that if the length of one of the sides is 1 unit, the perimeter would be 1+1+1+1 or 4 units.

Now draw two squares together as in the example below. Remind students that each side is still 1 unit long. Show them that the perimeter of this shape, a rectangle, would be 6 units.

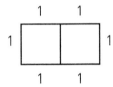

As a final demonstration, show them the "L" pentomino and ask them to find the perimeter. They should come up with 12 units.

Now tell them that they are going to make an island for the monsters using 4 pentominoes, and that they should try to make an island that has the greatest perimeter.

Have each child or group of children choose any 4 of the pentominoes. They will use the 4 shapes they have chosen to build the island. Because each pentomino has an area of 5 square units, every island they design using 4 pentominoes will have an area of exactly 20 square units.

Have them create islands with different perimeters, finding the design that has the greatest perimeter and trace their final solution on the accompanying grid. They should count and label the perimeter. They should also name their island, to make the activity more fun. There will invariably be multiple students who get the same perimeter but most will have different configurations.

To the left is a visual of how to find the perimeter of two pentominoes when they are joined together. To find the perimeter, just add the unit lengths around the shape. Each 1 to the left represents a side of length 1. Together these shapes have a perimeter of 16 units.

# Wild Thing Islands

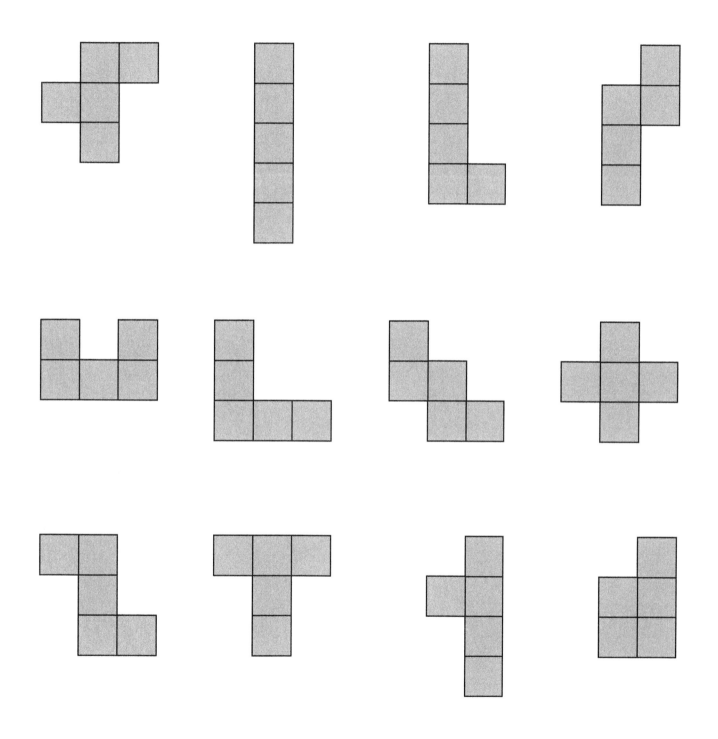

# Wild Thing Island Grid

## 3.OA.1
Interpret products of whole numbers, e.g., interpret 5 × 7 as the total number of objects in 5 groups of 7 objects each. *For example, describe a context in which a total number of objects can be expressed as 5 × 7.*

## 3.OA.2
Interpret whole-number quotients of whole numbers, e.g., interpret 56 ÷ 8 as the number of objects in each share when 56 objects are partitioned equally into 8 shares, or as a number of shares when 56 objects are partitioned into equal shares of 8 objects each. *For example, describe a context in which a number of shares or a number of groups can be expressed as 56 ÷ 8.*

## 3.OA.3
Use multiplication and division within 100 to solve word problems in situations involving equal groups, arrays, and measurement quantities, e.g., by using drawings and equations with a symbol for the unknown number to represent the problem.

## 3.OA.4
Determine the unknown whole number in a multiplication or division equation relating three whole numbers. *For example, determine the unknown number that makes the equation true in each of the equations 8 × ? = 48, 5 = _ ÷ 3, 6 × 6 = ?*

## 3.OA.6
Understand division as an unknown-factor problem. *For example, find 32 ÷ 8 by finding the number that makes 32 when multiplied by 8.*

## 3.OA.7
Fluently multiply and divide within 100, using strategies such as the relationship between multiplication and division (e.g., knowing that 8 × 5 = 40, one knows 40 ÷ 5 = 8) or properties of operations. By the end of Grade 3, know from memory all products of two one-digit numbers.

# Activity 5: The Wild Rumpus

Explain to students that you are going to do a series of activities based on the Wild Rumpus that Max and the Wild Things had.

Present this situation: Suppose Max wanted to calculate the amount of milk he needed for the party. Explain that Max decided that each of the 7 monsters would drink 3 cups of milk. Ask them to model the total number of cups they would need.

Have students either draw a picture showing a total of 21 cups or use a manipulative such as counters to model the situation.

Show them that they can think of this as 7 groups of 3: 3+3+3+3+3+3+3.

Now explain how we use multiplication to show this repeated addition: 7 x 3 means 7 groups of 3.

Also show them that they can think of the solution as 3 groups of 7: 7+7+7 or 3 x 7, which also equals 21.

This is an illustration of the commutative property.

Give students the following situation and ask them to create a model and then write the multiplication statement that represents it.

Other Wild Things decided to come to the party. 5 monsters came from another area of the island and each brought 4 lollipops to share with others at the party. What is the total number of lollipops they brought?

Create as many party scenarios as you feel are needed to reinforce this idea to your class. Different numbers of monsters can bring party hats, balloons, etc.

To assess student's ability to multiply or to use multiplication as repeated addition, give them the following problem and ask them to solve it by any means.

Max looked up and saw that there were now 10 monsters at the party. If they each had 4 lollipops, how many total lollipops would there be?

Explain to students that on the dance floor, there are 18 Wild Things.

If they need to pair up for a dance, how many pairs will there be? Again, have students model the situation either with manipulatives or with a drawing.

You may want to demonstrate that division can be accomplished by repeated subtraction. You can draw the 18 Wild Things on a board or tablet and cross off 2 at a time. Have the students count the number of times you cross off a pair until you get down to 0, that is no pairs left.

They will count 9 subtractions.

In other words, you will be saying: 18 - 2 = 16; 16 - 2 = 14; 14 - 2 = 12 .... 2 - 2 = 0

Students should come up with 9 pairs. Explain that this can be thought of with the following number sentence: $18 \div 2 = 9$

Another way to illustrate the concept of division is to draw 18 monsters and have students circle pairs. Show that you were able to separate the 18 monsters into 9 groups of 2.

Create as many party scenarios as you feel are needed to reinforce this idea to your class. Wild Things can form groups of 4 to bob for apples; they can leave the party in groups of 3, etc.

# RESOURCES

Sites that highlight high quality children's literature:

**The American Library Association**

www.ala.org

Their motto is: The best reading, for the largest number, at the least cost.

**Bank Street College of Education Children's Book Committee**
**The Best Children's Books of the Year Five to Nine**

https://s3.amazonaws.com/bankstreet_web/media/filer_public/2012/04/30/2012fivetonine.pdf

Bank Street College of Education strives to guide librarians, educators, parents, grandparents and other interested adults to the best books for children published each year.

**Kirkus Reviews**

www.kirkusreviews.com/book-reviews/childrens-books

Lists of all book reviews are available on their website.

**School Library Journal**

www.schoollibraryjournal.com

An extensive publication, their web site reviews all media.

**Seven Impossible Things Before Breakfast: A blog about books**

www.sevenimpossiblethings.org

Read the blog of Julie Walker Danielson to keep in tune with what's happening in the world of children's literature.

Sites that are helpful for planning mathematics activities:

**The National Council of Teachers of Mathematics (NCTM) Illuminations**

www.illuminations.nctm.org

**The National Library of Virtual Manipulatives**

www.nlvm.usu.edu

# INDEX

# AUTHORS

Adam Goldberg, Ed.D., is an Associate Professor of Mathematics Education at Southern Connecticut State University, where he focuses on mathematics for current and future elementary teachers. Of particular interest to Adam is the integration of literature, technology, and manipulatives in the mathematics classroom. He lives in Connecticut with his wife Kerri and daughter Isobel.

Maria Diamantis, Ed.D., is a Professor of Mathematics Education at Southern Connecticut State University. She has taught mathematics content and methods courses for pre-service and in-service teachers for the past 17 years, and has presented workshops that integrate mathematics, science, literature, and social studies for grades K-6 at the national, regional, and statewide levels. She is interested in mathematics critical thinking, and problem solving in the K-6 curriculum using integration to other disciplines.

© 2011 Stephanie Anestis
Photography

M.W. Penn is an award winning author of 15 children's picture books focused on mathematics and an award winning poet. Her poetry is published in Highlights for Children magazine and several anthologies. She presents sessions in interdisciplinary literature at NCTM and NCTE conferences across the country. Visit her website **www.mwpenn.com**.

CPSIA information can be obtained
at www.ICGtesting.com
Printed in the USA
BVOW11s1530140517
483977BV00007B/14/P